THE HALLOWEEN HANDBOOK

ALIEN
page 2

GYPSY
page 13

GODDESS
page 11

PLAYBOY
BUNNY
page 7

HIPPIE
page 13

DEVIL IN A
BLUE DRESS
page 8

MUMMY
page 15

chapter 1 **Classics and Classics with a Twist**

BLACK-EYED
SUSAN
page 27

SHOOTING STAR
page 43

CHICK
MAGNET
page 32

GOLD DIGGER
page 34

POINTLESS
page 41

WEB SURFER
page 46

chapter 2 **Play with Your Words**

BATHING BEAUTY
page 48

CHIPPENDALE'S DANCER
page 52

CARMEN MIRANDA
page 64

GOD'S GIFT TO WOMEN
page 59

STRIPPER EMERGING FROM A CAKE
page 66

JAZZ SINGER
page 63

chapter 3 **Come-Hither Costumes**

THOMAS AQUINAS
page 70

QUEEN ELIZABETH
page 81

1980s GIRL
page 86

JULIUS CAESAR
page 72

CASTRO
page 79

FLAPPER
page 84

chapter 4 **History in the Making**

HOLLY GOLIGHTLY
page 102

JUDY JETSON
page 103

DOUBLEMINT TWINS
page 120

GOT MILK?
page 121

HAMBURGER
HELPER
page 121

chapter 5 **Movie and TV Characters**

TINA TURNER
page 138

JACKIE
KENNEDY
ONASSIS
page 135

AXL ROSE
page 136

EVEL KNIEVEL
page 133

MICK JAGGER
page 132

JANE GOODALL
page 130

chapter 6 **Celeb Sightings**

chapter 7 **Literature and Arts**

chapter 8 **The Sporting Life**

chapter 9 **Crowd Participation**

chapter 10 **Around the World**

chapter 11 For the Group

chapter 12 A Movable Feast

MONOPOLY MAN
page 224

ROBOT
page 227

BRIDEZILLA
page 216

HEAD ON
A SILVER
PLATTER
page 220

JELLYFISH
page 223

HOT-AIR
BALLOON
page 221

chapter 13 **Odds and Ends**

CLOWN
page 243

PETER
PAN
page 245

PRINCESS
page 245

BUTTON
page 252

TINKERBELL
page 250

chapter 14 **Nursery Rhymes, Fairy Tales, and Costumes for the Young at Heart**

THE HALLOWEEN HANDBOOK

447 COSTUMES

by BRIDIE CLARK and ASHLEY DODD

Costume photos by JANETTE BECKMAN

WORKMAN PUBLISHING ★ NEW YORK

To our mothers, Kathe Dodd and Margy Clark, for their incredible support, enthusiasm, and example.

Cataloging-in-Publication Data is available from the Library of Congress.

ISBN 0-7611-2987-1

Workman books are available at special discounts when purchased in bulk for premiums and sales promotions as well as for fund-raising or educational use. Special editions or book excerpts can also be created to specification. For details, contact the Special Sales Director at the address below.

Workman Publishing Company, Inc.
708 Broadway
New York, NY 10003-9555

www.workman.com

Printed in the United States of America

First printing August 2004

10 9 8 7 6 5 4 3 2 1

Contents

THE COSTUME ENCYCLOPEDIA

1. CLASSICS AND CLASSICS WITH A TWIST 1

BUNNY
page 7

2. PLAY WITH YOUR WORDS . . . 25

CEREAL KILLER
page 31

3. COME-HITHER COSTUMES . . 47

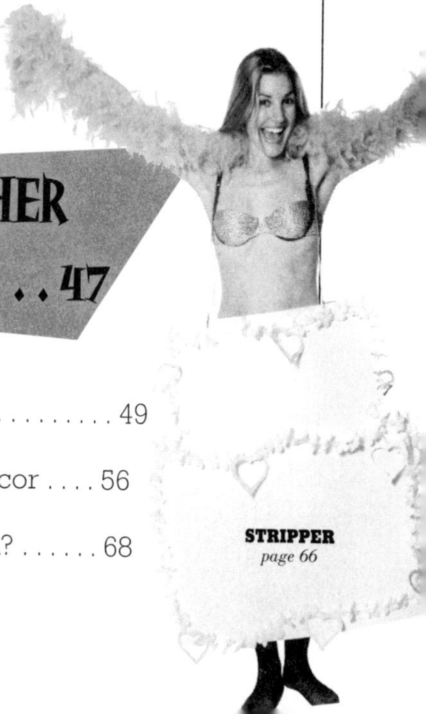

STRIPPER
page 66

FIDEL CASTRO
page 79

DOUBLEMINT TWINS
page 120

TINA TURNER
page 138

HANNIBAL LECHTER
page 124

JACKSON POLLOCK PAINTING
page 153

EXTRA POINT
page 161

Dear Readers,

Minus one extremely itchy night in a Mom-made Care Bear costume (Bridie) and an unfortunate episode as a misunderstood California Raisin (Ashley), Halloween has always been our favorite holiday.

Why? As kids, it had most to do with the pillowcase full of candy. But as adults, whose wardrobes look like STUDIES IN GRAY AND BLACK, there's the promise of a night of completely imaginative dress-up—of a night spent as a Princess, a Pop Icon from the '70s, or a character from a book. It's a "kid-again" kind of experience. (And there's still the easy access to copious amounts of chocolate—never a bad thing.)

We love Halloween. And yet, even we must confess: Despite our unbridled enthusiasm for the holiday, there HAVE been years when October 31 seemed to sneak up quickly, leaving us in a scramble to come up with something cute to wear. So for those similarly in need of inspiration, we've compiled a gallery of around 450 of the most creative and memorable Halloween costumes. Our promise: You'll never be stuck without a clever costume idea again. And we haven't left the kids out—we've included costume ideas for little people, as well as parent–child combos that are adorable and fun to create. You'll also find makeup tips, costume recycling ideas, and other suggestions to help you celebrate Halloween in style.

Ashley as Raisin   *Bridie as Care Bear*

And for all the Halloween junkies who want to know more about the history of the holiday—and how all the traditions we associate with October 31 have become woven together throughout the centuries—we'll fill you in as we go along.

May your Halloweens be fun-filled and your candy sacks weighty!

Trick or treat,

Ashley & Bridie

THE HISTORY OF HALLOWEEN

As a kid, your parents explained the origins of your family's traditions and religious celebrations. Your teachers told you everything you needed to know about the first Thanksgiving. You might even have a vague recollection about when and why Arbor Day was established. But did anyone ever bother to fill you in on the history of Halloween? We're guessing the answer is nope, nary a lesson on the uniquely *weird* (and, admittedly, rather murky) origins of our mainstream modern holiday.

This year, rather than just donning your Halloween garb and heading to a costume party, make up for lost time and get some Halloween education between your ears.

Approximately 350 B.C.E.: Ancient Celts, who lived in the area that is now Ireland, the United Kingdom, and northern France, marked the end of summer and the advent of cold, harsh winter with the biggest celebration of their year, the festival of **Samhein** (pronounced sow-in). On **October 31,** they believed that ancestral ghosts returned to the living world. It was also the day when the spirits of those who had died during the year were able to travel to the underworld. Some of these ghosts and spirits were friendly guests, for whom the believers lit paths and set out plates on the table. Other souls were far less gracious, wreaking havoc on crops and generally causing mischief, and some were even believed to demonically "possess" the bodies of the living, forcing them to do their bidding.

But all of these otherworldly visitors, whether good or destructive, had some upside: The Celts credited them with enabling Druid priests to predict the future with enhanced clarity. Faced with a long, potentially terminal winter, these prophecies were essential for keeping up the Celtic morale. To honor the arrival of both the spirits and the winter, the priests built enormous bonfires, and revelers burned crops and animals as sacrifices to their

THREE BLIND MICE, *page 244*

gods. They also dressed up—usually as animals, in pelts and heads—and later, after the party had died down, relit their own fires with flaming torches taken from the sacred communal **bonfire.**

First century C.E.: The Romans were the new show in town, and stayed put as rulers for the next 400 years. During this reign, they mixed the Samhein festival with two of their own: **Feralia,** a day which commemorated the passing of the dead, and **Pomona,** a day on which they paid homage to the goddess of fruit and trees. Since the Pomona was symbolized by the apple, many believe that this new synthesis of festivals originated our tradition of **bobbing for apples.**

Fourth century C.E.: Constantine the Great proclaimed **Christianity** to be the new religion of the Roman Empire, effectively ending the open practice of

Samhein and other paleo-pagan traditions. The Druids, once revered, became a heavily persecuted group, and often faced execution.

Ninth century: Christianity's widespread influence throughout Celtic lands meant that pagan festivals for the dead and undead were deemed a no-no. Instead, Pope Gregory IV decreed that November 1 would be **All Saints' Day,** a church-sanctioned holiday to honor saints and martyrs.

Eleventh century: The Catholic Church designated November 2 as All Souls' Day to commemorate the dead, and celebrated with bonfires, parades, revelry, and **costumes.** During the festival, poor citizens in England begged families for pastries called **soul cakes,** and in exchange promised to pray for the family's dearly departed. This practice, called going a-souling, was eventually

The Etymology of "Bonfire"

The Celts didn't call their big blazes bonfires. Bonfires were actually *bone-fires,* referring to the sacrificial burning of animals (and their bones) during Samhein. The Celts also disposed of human remains on a funeral pyre, a spiritual practice with the practical advantage of helping prevent the rampant spread of diseases. Over the centuries, the word *bon* (French for good) was swapped for *bone*—leaving us with a cozy conception of a bonfire, and a modern meaning divorced from its pagan origins.

Bobbing for Apples and Other Apple Divinations

An apple a day . . . helps predict your future? Seems a little far-fetched, but it's true that apples have been used for centuries as a prediction tool, and in particular as a way of determining how one's love life will turn out. If a girl peels an apple in one long, unbroken strip, for example, and then leaves the peel in a bowl of water, it was believed that the peel would form the first initial of her future husband's first name. And here's an old-fashioned game for a girl with many potential boyfriends: She slices the apple open and sticks the wet seeds to her face, naming one for each suitor. The seed that drops off first indicates a would-be boyfriend who'd turn out to be a no-good cheat. The last seed on her face will be her next love.

And bobbing for apples, that classic Halloween party game, was also used to predict the future. According to the Victorians, the first young person to pluck an apple from the tub of icy water without using his or her hands would be the first to marry.

If you want to try to influence destiny, here are a few tips for better bobbing success. Look at the selection of apples in the tub and choose the one that looks the smallest. (The smaller the apple, the easier it will be to get your mouth around it.) Once you've chosen the perfect apple, there are two proven methods for capturing it. Either push it with your mouth to one of the tub's surfaces (the bottom, a side, or a corner) and pin it there; or go for a quick kill and duck your head in as fast as you can. The apple won't know what hit it.

For those concerned about potential germs from sticking your face into a tub of water and apples that others have already bobbed, you can still exercise your apple-bobbing skills by modifying the game a bit.

Instead of putting your apples in a tub of water, tie a ribbon or string around the apples' stems, then use thumbtacks to hang them from the top of a door frame. Let each player zero in on one apple, and just like bobbing, the first person to get a hold of his or her apple (again, no hands!) wins. When a player is unsuccessful, cut his or her apple down and present it as a consolation prize.

adopted by neighborhood children who solicited food, money, and ale.

Seventeenth century:

Very little Halloween action going on with the rigid **Puritans** (in fact, there wasn't much celebrating of any kind with these guys—Christmas and Easter were nixed, too), but settlers in Maryland and other southern colonies brought their varied traditions with them and meshed them with gusto in the New World. A distinctly American Halloween tradition was soon forged: Public celebrations were held to rejoice over the harvest, and neighbors would gather to swap ghost stories, tell each other's fortunes, and revel in the new season.

Mid-nineteenth century:

The influx of immigrants to the United States, particularly the nearly two million Irish fleeing the potato famine, brought the celebration of Halloween to a national scale. Americans, drawing from Irish traditions,

started dressing in costumes and going door-to-door getting treats from their neighbors.

Late nineteenth century:

Halloween began to evolve into a festive community event, with the grotesque or scary elements of the tradition downplayed. This paved the way for our twentieth-century secular, mass-market celebration of the holiday.

And that brings us to the present, in which Halloween has been transformed into a multibillion-dollar industry, with display cases and entire stores dedicated to pushing factory-made costumes on millions of Americans. A few people might nostalgically note that, as a society, we've lost touch with the original meaning of Halloween. Call us unsentimental, but the earliest celebrations of Halloween were premised on the firmly held belief that the dead came back to earth one night a year to potentially snatch and possess the bodies of the living. Thanks, but no thanks— we'll take snack-size Milky Ways over that scene any day!

We *are* a bit nostalgic, though, about those costumes that mom lovingly whipped up out of nothing. So now that you're better versed in Halloween history, it's time for you to create something for yourself. Start strategizing your perfect costume with a few hundred of our favorite ideas. Browse through our stellar selection of getups, and allow them to inspire your creative impulses. Halloween is the one night a year when you can reinvent yourself completely without your friends and family doubting your sanity. Choose a character from your favorite book, think back to your childhood idol, or become that historical person you *always* based your school reports on. Spend a little time brain-storming, then get to it!

We designed these low-budget, easy-to-make-from-stuff-around-the-house costumes with the hope that you'll have almost as much fun *preparing* for your costume party as you'll have being there. To start, search the deepest depths of your closet. Yup, that's right. As dark and scary as it may be, you never know what gem could turn up. For example, remember that hideous zebra print muumuu your grandmother gave you because she thought it was "so sweet," but which never saw the light of day? It's time to drag it out!

Young Ashley masters the perfect cheer.

If, however, you're one of those organized people who manages to clean the closets once a year (Who are you, and where do you come from?), you'll have to reclaim other people's diamonds in the rough. Secondhand stores and Salvation Army stores are treasure troves for putting together unique costumes. Anything from '80s tennis outfits to bridesmaid dresses can be found there for a few dollars. The Halloween hunt is on!

Remember that you can collect goodies year-round. You might not know in March what your Halloween costume will be, but keep your eyes and your mind open. Some costumes, for example, call for gold or silver clothing. If a shimmery metallic look is you, stock up whenever you see it. That silver shirt you saw in the spring might be gone by October.

Zeus gets his wish.

Classics and Classics with a Twist

What's wrong with tried-and-true? Here's a refresher course on some old standbys—plus a few new ideas to switch things up.

ALIEN

For an out-of-this-world costume, go as a classically retro **alien:**

Gather up whatever silver clothing you can find and some go-go boots. Get yourself a silver space gun, and make or buy a headband with little antennae sticking out. Cover any exposed areas with green body paint (see opposite for a body paint recipe). Bring a cell phone so that you can "phone home" whenever you feel the longing.

Alien-a-go-go

How to Make Face (or Body) Paint

There's nothing wrong with store-bought greasepaint, but for the hard-core types who want to make their own, we offer this simple recipe.

You'll need:

- **2 tablespoons shortening**
- **5 teaspoons cornstarch**
- **1 tablespoon white flour**
- **3 to 4 drops glycerin (available at any drugstore)**
- **food coloring**
- **cold cream (we like Pond's)**
- **Q-tips and makeup sponges**

Thoroughly mix the shortening, cornstarch, and flour until it forms a paste. Add the glycerin and stir again until the mixture becomes smooth and easy to spread. Add food coloring a drop at a time until you get the color you like.

Use the Q-tips to create patterns—rainbows, stars, scars, freckles—you name it. If you're painting the entire face, remember to blend into the hairline a bit, and don't forget your neck and ears. (Hands, cleavage, arms, and legs should also be painted to add the needed authenticity to certain looks. The Incredible Hulk, for example, can't give a pale handshake, and a sexy devil better be red in all the places her low-cut shirt doesn't cover.) For cleanup afterwards, we advocate patience—it *will* come off—and tons of cold cream.

ANGEL

Whether or not you're an angel in real life, you can be one this Halloween . . . and there are lots of variations from which to choose.

■ There's your **basic angel.** You'll need long, white, flowing vestments (any white dress or suit will do), sandals, a golden halo, a trumpet or harp (real ones are heavy and expensive—buy a toy one or construct one out of cardboard and string and paint it gold), and, of course, some wings (see opposite).

■ Add crutches, wrap your arm in an Ace bandage, and you're a **fallen angel.**

■ Take the most scintillating page from the Victoria's Secret catalog, and go for the **sexy angel** look (always a favorite). You'll need red lingerie or black leather, faux fur, and wings.

■ To be a **Hell's Angel,** throw on your beat-up, oversized black leather jacket, Harley-Davidson T-shirt, ripped jeans, red bandanna, beard, and gold hoop earring. If anyone asks, your hog's parked outside.

■ Or get animated . . . remember how cartoon characters, when whipsawed by a moment of moral debate, would suddenly find a **tiny angel** perched on one shoulder and a **tiny devil** on the other? Get a friend to dress up as Lucifer (page 8), and deck yourself out as his or her better half. Help fellow partygoers make the right decisions.

Winging It

What angel, fairy, or butterfly is complete without a set of wings? Here are a few ways to make your costume take flight.

An economical, but time-consuming approach is to create the wings yourself. It's easy and might not even require a trip to the store, depending on what you have lying around your house. You can make translucent, ethereal wings out of panty hose or a more bare-bones pair out of poster board.

For the gossamer wings, you'll need panty hose and 9-gauge wire or coat hangers. First, twist the wire into a figure eight and bind the middle by twisting the metal two or three times. Feel free to create your own variation in shape or size to accommodate your costume's needs. (For example, demon wings are shaped differently than butterfly wings.)

Next, pull a leg of the panty hose over each wing and tie the extra material in the middle. You can also use polyester organza—easily found at any fabric store—to cover the wire frame. Again tie the extra material in the middle. Consider buying glitter cloth paint at a craft store to decorate your wings.

To wear your panty-hose wings, get a friend to pin them to your upper back.

In a rush? Quickly make a set of wings by using a pencil to sketch your desired wing shape onto a piece of white poster board, and cut it out. Two feet is a good length for a single wing, but feel free to make yours larger or smaller, depending on your costume and your preference. Next, trace and cut out the same pattern on a second piece of poster board. Use a hole punch to make two holes on the flat edge of each wing, and tie them together (ribbon is sturdy and prettier than twine) and then around your shoulders and waist—like a backpack. Silver glitter adds a touch of the ephemeral: First use spray glue to coat the wings, or a glue stick to make patterns or outline your wings' edges, then add glitter.

Another option is to buy your wings at a costume shop. They're available in many different sizes, shapes, and colors. The basic white, black, and red wings are usually made out of feathers, and most of the fairy and insect wings are made out of sheer nylon over wire. If you don't have the time, energy, or patience to create your own wings, there's no shame in plunking down money for them. Prices vary, but as the saying goes, you get what you pay for.

BAT

After witches, ghosts, and black cats, nothing says Halloween more than a sinister **black bat.** You can easily make bat ears out of a black headband, glue, and felt, or take the easy way out and buy costume ears. Dress all in black, don a black cape, and paint your face black, too. Then use safety pins to secure the sides of the cape to your arms. When your arms are down, your wings are folded; open them wide and you're ready to fly! Add some fangs to become a **vampire bat.**

Chew on This: Faux Fangs

If you're looking to increase your costume's scare-factor, consider investing in a shocking smile. Custom-fit porcelain fangs are a bone-chilling addition to any costume—especially for vampire, demon, or zombie getups. Made from the same material as dentures, the fangs are created to fit the unique shape of your mouth, and even match the natural color of your teeth! The result is a heart-stopping, realistic quality. Although they're a bit pricey (approximately $100), you may decide that the petrified look on your friends' faces is worth the cost. To check out fang designs and prices go to: **www.teethbydnash.com** or **www.vampfangs.net.**

BRIDE AND GROOM

The basic costumes are obvious—white dress, veil, and bouquet for her, tuxedo for him. But here's the twist: Both the bride and the groom wrap a six-foot length of rope around their waists, and when asked why they have a spare piece of rope trailing from one side, each finds the other to **tie the knot.** A little hokey, we know, but if both of you take nervous draws from a flask (to help calm prewedding jitters), you won't feel embarrassed for long.

BUNNY

Dress in a pink or white long-sleeve leotard with matching tights and attach a fluffy ball of cotton to your rear end. Wear matching sneakers or high heels. Add whiskers (drawn on your face with eyeliner pencil), store-bought rabbit ears, and a carrot, and you're ready to get the party hopping.

■ Add a drum, some sticks, and a pair of shades, and you're the **Energizer Bunny.**

■ Grab a basketful of dyed or chocolate eggs and you're . . . you guessed it, the **Easter Bunny.**

■ For a sexy bunny variation, replace the pink or white getup with a black leotard, sheer stockings, and high heels. Add a bow tie, white wrist cuffs, and a white tail. To get further inspiration for your **Playboy Bunny,** see **Hugh Hefner,** page 61.

■ Get a bunch of friends dressed as a variety of bunnies together, and you're a **bunny hutch!**

■ Four friends can vary the standard rabbit costume slightly to dress as **Peter Rabbit** (in a light blue jacket) and **Flopsy, Mopsy,** and **Cottontail** (in red cloaks).

■ Add leggings, snow boots, and a warm winter jacket and you're a **snow bunny.**

DEVIL

Feeling devilish this Halloween? You know how to get the **Lucifer** look. (Dress all in red, with a cape, horns, a pitchfork, and a tail. Paint your face red, add thick black eyeliner and lipstick.

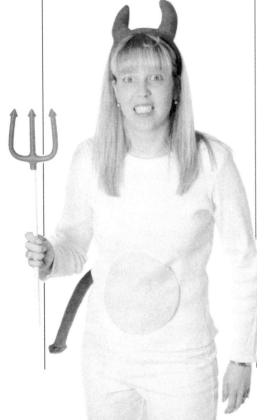

Trace your eyebrows into high arches using black eyeliner. Add fake contacts for an especially satanic look.) But let's be honest: Going as plain old Satan—*yawn.* Why not spruce up the costume by tweaking it just a bit?

■ Lose the red clothing and throw on a little blue frock to become the **devil in a blue dress** (right). (Keep the horns, pitchfork, tail, etc.) You must have been sent from . . . below? If you're mistaken for Monica Lewinsky, so much the better.

■ Put on the old Lucifer horns, carry the pitchfork, but wear an all-white outfit. Affix a yellow felt or paper oval to your stomach. You're a **deviled egg** (left).

■ And yet another devil variation: You're all in red, you've got the pitchfork and the tail. Now strap on a pair of roller skates, and you're **hell on wheels.**

FRANKENSTEIN

Yes, we've read the Mary Shelley classic, and we know that Frankenstein is the scientist and not the monster, but popular culture is winning this battle. Paint yourself a shade of green, pull your hair back, and paint your lips black. Wear a white oxford shirt that's a size or two too small, and a black blazer with sleeves that end at your forearm. Black pants should be high-waters, black shoes should be big and clunky. Adopt a stagger. Snarl. Paint your fingernails with black nail polish.

Here's how to make the neck bolts that presumably keep your head from rolling off your shoulders. Carefully cut a wine bottle cork in half and paint it silver. Now simply fasten both halves to either side of your neck with cosmetic adhesive.

Grab a friend to go as the **Bride of Frankenstein.** She should wear a wedding dress and whip her hair up into a beehive of gravity-defying proportions, with a lightning bolt pattern in white up each side. A beehive hairdo requires a lot of curling and teasing and tons of hairspray: Just keep making your hair bigger and bigger and taller and taller. To create a white lightning bolt, use a half-inch paintbrush to paint white greasepaint onto each side of your 'do.

Note: Guys who have spent a little extra time at the gym in recent months might want to consider going as the buffer **Incredible Hulk.** Costume is the same as Frankenstein's, just ditch the shirt and the silver bolts.

Stuck on You: Adhering Things to Your Skin

Please don't use superglue or regular adhesive to attach things such as mustaches, Frankenstein bolts, warts, or anything else to your skin. Those glues weren't designed for skin contact, and they're likely to cause lots of irritation—especially when you try to remove whatever it is that you've stuck to yourself. Instead, pick up some spirit gum (and remover) at a costume or Halloween shop.

GLADIATOR

Yes, we realize that some men might be deterred by the prospect of wearing a skirt, no matter how

Real men do wear skirts.

masculine the costume. But for those who refuse to be slaves to strict gender roles, put on a short brown skirt, soccer shin pads painted brown, and sandals. Grab a mighty toy sword, brush your (short) hair forward onto your forehead (like a Caesar cut), and you're sure to win the adulation of the crowd. Construct a breastplate by taking a piece of cardboard that's about the same shape as your upper body and covering it with tinfoil.

"Son of Scotland, I am William Wallace."

Cut two holes at each shoulder and fasten over each arm using string. For braver hearts, expose those gams in a plaid kilt and you'll be a **highland warrior.** Wear a simple brown T-shirt and brown boots, wrap a tartan over your shoulders, let your long hair down, and carry a sword or a bow and arrow.

GODDESS

Getting in touch with your inner **goddess** is all well and good, but don't forget your neglected outer one. Give *her* some time—after all, she's got the power to reduce mortal men to doddering fools.

Make your lightning bolt first. Step 1: Sketch out a lightning bolt pattern on a large sheet of cardboard (use a ruler). Step 2: Cut out the pattern. Step 3: Paint entirely gold, let dry, and then glue on lots of gold glitter. Alternate Step 3: Cover your cardboard bolt entirely with aluminum foil, pressing around the edges of the board. Repeat until you have a hefty bolt.

Now for your dress. You'll need some white fabric (patterns are *très gauche* on Mount Olympus) and some thick gold cord, available at your local sewing

or trimmings shop. Drape, wrap, or tie it to yourself any way you like. Our favorite version of a toga is as simple as it is sexy. First, hold up your fabric with both hands. It should be a little longer than your arm span. Wrap it around your back, and under your armpits like a strapless

dress with the bulk of the fabric in the front. Now, take the top left and right edge. Cross them over each other, so you have two folds of fabric on your chest. Take the ends and tie them behind your neck—securely (need we emphasize?). Use the gold cord to cinch material around your waist, and for added effect, lace it up your arms and calves. The result will be supremely flattering—and you won't reveal more of yourself than mortal laws allow. On your feet, sandals are best unless it's just too chilly for bare toes. In that case, improvise. True goddesses, after all, remain flexible.

Add some gold glitter down your arm and a dusting in the décolletage, and you've got yourself some divine aura, girl! Head to the makeup aisle of your local drugstore around Halloween, and you'll find an abundance of the gilded, powdery stuff. Make a crown of laurels for your head (anything viney from a craft store or florist will do) or, if that's not around, just use some more gold cord.

Goddess Variations

Take the basic goddess getup and add a special prop to take your place among the Greek pantheon.

ATHENA

WHO	WHAT SHE WAS KNOWN FOR	HOW YOU CAN PORTRAY HER
Aphrodite	Goddess of Love and Beauty	Hand out Hershey Kisses, safety-pin red and pink felt hearts to your toga
Artemis	Goddess of the Hunt	Carry a toy bow and arrows
Athena	Goddess of Wisdom	Attach a plastic or plush toy owl to your wrist or shoulder
Demeter	Goddess of Agriculture and Fertility	Carry symbols of each of the seasons in a basket (a winter scarf, a bunch of flowers, a beach ball, an apple)
Pandora	First Mortal Female	Carry an open box
Persephone	Goddess of the Underworld	Carry a pomegranate

GYPSY

Going as a **gypsy** is tried-and-true. The long flowing skirt, the leather boots, the gold hoop earrings, the bandanna tied tightly around the head, scarves around the shoulders and waist, the heavy eye makeup. It works, but why not make it more fun with audience participation? Carry around a magic eight ball, and ask people if they'd like their fortunes told or their palms read.

Q: Why did the gypsy give up fortune telling?
A: She couldn't see a future in it.

HIPPIE

Feeling groovy? Throw on your best **hippie** threads and keep it mellow. Bell-bottoms are crucial for both sexes. Girls should go for a blousy peasant top, guys for a butterfly-collared paisley print. Don a pair of John Lennon–style wire-rimmed glasses. Part hair in the middle. Paint peace signs on your cheeks or carry a MAKE LOVE, NOT WAR protest sign.

ISLAND CASTAWAY

Wear some tattered, ripped clothing (your pants legs should be two different lengths), grow a beard (or attach a fake one with spirit gum), and mess up your hair. Other "Survivor" touches: a message in a glass bottle and a coconut with a straw in it (for your beverage of choice).

MERMAID

Our friend Elizabeth recalls a particularly happy Halloween at age ten, when she and her little sister dressed up in matching, homemade **mermaid** costumes. Here's how they did it. First: Out of green felt, they constructed long, cylindrical skirts that got skinnier at the ankles. Second: They each cut a crescent-moon shape out of cardboard, covered it with aluminum foil, and attached it to the bottom and back of the skirt. Third: They covered two of their mom's old bikini tops with aluminum foil, adding shell necklaces to complete the ensemble.

MIME

Feeling antisocial? Deck out in whiteface (with dark brows and eyeliner), white gloves, and all black clothing, and others will guess your new identity without you having to say a word. And should you encounter a fellow partygoer with whom you don't even want a silent exchange, pantomime your invisible wall and walk away.

MUMMY

You won't win points for originality, but you can easily pull together a **mummy** costume with household supplies: Tear up an old white sheet into long strips (if you don't have an extra, look for one at a thrift store), or just use gauze and/or toilet paper. Wrap your bandages around a tight, all-white outfit, (keeping things loose at your knees, waist, shoulders, and elbows), fasten with white medical or duct tape, and you're back from the dead.

NEANDERTHAL

Take a few steps back in the evolutionary process. Smudge a little "dirt" (brown eye shadow or blush) on your face. Wear a ragged-looking minitoga (see page 11) of leopard print or brown fabric, put on your earthiest leather sandals, and carry a club or a rudimentary slingshot. Mess up your hair. Walk with a slouch. Grunt. You've gone back to your **Neanderthal** roots.

VAMPIRE

The standard **vampire** getup is a long black cape, all black garb, and a very pale face. Get some realistic and terrifying fangs (see page 6). Lips should be a dull grayish purple. Drip fake blood from one side of your mouth but don't paint it on; instead, put a bit of fake blood in your mouth, stand over the sink, and let it drip down your chin—it will look more natural. With a black eyebrow or eyeliner pencil, define eyebrows so that they arch sharply and villainously. Pick up some red or black contact lenses if you can. Slick your hair back or part it in the middle and then slick it back.

For a vamp variation, try **Count Chocula.** Who doesn't understand, on certain days, craving chocolate so badly that you're convinced you'll die without it? Dress in a brown suit and tie a brown cape around your shoulders. Carry Hershey bars in both hands.

Q: Who is a vampire most likely to fall in love with?

A: The girl necks door.

How to Make Fake Blood

Couldn't be simpler: All you need is corn syrup and red food coloring. But be forewarned, any kind of fake blood, whether homemade or store-bought, *will* stain your clothes.

Here's Looking at You: Fashion Contact Lenses

We hesitate to share the following information, because frankly, this terrifying trend scares the living daylights out of us. But that is, for some, a central goal of dressing up for Halloween, so here goes: **fashion contact lenses.** Not particularly scary sounding, you say? Just wait 'til you're at a crowded Halloween party and you notice a nice-looking young vampire across the room. The two of you make eye contact— and his (or her) eyes are a bright, blazing, totally frightening shade of red. OK . . . who invited Satan? Well, chances are (though we make no guarantees) your vampire is wearing fake lenses. You can find red, black, wolflike, catlike, and pupil-less contacts at **www.colorfulcontacts.com** or **www.evileyes.com.** This touch adds an edge of eerie realism to any vampire or demon.

Going Batty for Vampires

An undead Brad Pitt.

When the Irish author Bram Stoker published *Dracula* in 1897, he probably didn't expect his bloodthirsty yet distinguished Count to affect the world the way he did. Even today, more than a century later, the vampire craze continues in full force. Dracula and his modern kin saturate popular media through movies, television series, cartoons, video games, novels, and even comic books. So what's the profile of the pale ones?

Vampires are the living dead. They sleep in coffins during the day, and awake to feed at night. They subsist on human blood, piercing the necks of their victims with their two sharp fangs. They possess the strength of twenty men, can shape-shift into bats or wolves, and don't cast reflections or shadows. Thankfully, vampires can't enter a home without being invited, and they're deterred by garlic, holy water, and crucifixes. The only way to kill a vampire is to expose him to sunlight or pierce his heart with a wooden stake.

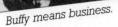

Buffy means business.

Of course, this is just a general description. The habits, capabilities, and weaknesses of vampires are constantly being redefined. From the 1931 production of *Dracula* starring Bela Lugosi to the 1994 production of *Interview with the Vampire* starring Brad Pitt and Tom Cruise (based on Anne Rice's 1976 novel) and beyond, the Western image of vampires has been reinvented and revisualized for years. It could be argued that of all the boogeymen of Halloween, vampires are the most versatile. From silly to sexy, these fanged fiends fit any bill. Their admirers span from the *Sesame Street* set watching Count Von Count, to the teen and young adult crowd following the supernatural suspense television series *Buffy the Vampire Slayer* or *Angel*.

Romanian Roots

The real-life inspiration for the central figure in Bram Stoker's novel was Prince Vlad Tepes, who lived in the mid 1400s in the Carpathian Mountains of Transylvania, Romania. This Romanian prince was given the honorific title *Dracula,* meaning *son of the dragon,* because his father had been of the Order of the Dragon, dedicated to keeping the Turks and heretics from taking over Romanian lands. Of course, Vlad Tepes did not embody any qualities of a vampire, but his rule was certainly a bloody one. Widely known as a sadist, Vlad Tepes used terrifying tactics to protect his land from Turkish invaders and the Ottoman rule. In addition to impaling the heads of more than 20,000 Turkish men, women, and children on stakes as a warning to further invaders, other equally gruesome accounts of Vlad's reigns cause historians to believe that he was responsible for the deaths of as many as 100,000 people.

Despite these unimaginable deeds, the original Dracula never drank human blood or turned himself into a bat—at least from what we know. Then again, it was rumored that when Vlad Tepes's gravesite was exhumed in the 1930s, no body was found.

WEREWOLF

Is that a full moon? Transform yourself into a terrifying werewolf by adhering faux fur (see page 9) on your cheeks and hands. Use an eye pencil to slant your eyebrows so they meet in the middle and smudge brown makeup on the rest of your face. Buy fake werewolf ear tips. Wear a shaggy brown sweater and brown pants, and gel your hair up so that you look like a creature of the wild. Fake fangs (see page 6) are the last necessary ingredient. For a variation, bring back Michael J. Fox's **Teen Wolf.** Puberty's never easy, but it's especially tough when a full moon makes you break out in fur and fangs. Add to the teen element with a varsity letterman's jacket, high school sweatshirt, or something along those adolescent lines.

Q: Why are werewolves considered quick-witted?

A: Because they always give snappy answers.

Accessing Extra Accessories

No matter how thrifty your homemade costumes are, there are times when the perfect finishing touch is something that must be bought, like a set of Austin Powers's teeth, or werewolf ear tips. Or maybe you're the noncreative type and making your own wings or monster feet is your idea of a nightmare. Or you're really short on time. Don't fret! Head out to the mall or your local Halloween shop and find the cherry for your sundae. If you have the time to wait for a shipment and you'd rather shop online, here are some Web sites to check out:

- **www.halloweenmart.com**
- **www.costumesinc.com**
- **www.allcostumes.com**
- **www.frightcatalog.com**
- **www.extremehalloween. com**

The Wherefore of Werewolves

The wolf is "the eternal symbol for ferocity and inordinate evil appetite," wrote Reverend Montague Summers in his 1933 tome, *The Werewolf.* It's common knowledge these days that werewolves are men and women who turn into wolves under the full moon to feast on animals and people, only to resume their human form at daybreak. While these sharp-toothed shape-shifters have howled their way into Hollywood scripts, suspense novels, and nightmares for decades, where did the werewolf's legend *originally* begin? According to European folklore, the werewolf population was alarmingly high in sixteenth-century France and England, with Paris and London as the true hot spots for these hairy creatures.

Here are some helpful hints in case you ever find yourself being pursued by a four-legged beast during the full moon.

FULL MOON FACTS

How does someone become a werewolf?

- **Eating the brain of a werewolf**
- **Drinking from the same source as a werewolf**
- **Getting bitten by a werewolf**

How can you tell if someone is a werewolf while they are still in their human form? They'll have:

- **Hairy or rough palms**
- **Tattoos of the crescent moon on their body**
- **Slanted eyebrows that meet in the middle**
- **A noticeably longer third finger on each hand**

WITCH

What would Halloween be without witches? And the great thing is there are so many fun (and easy) variations. To conjure up a classic witch like **Broom-Hilda** or **The Wicked Witch of the West,** wear a long black dress or skirt and shirt and black boots. Cover face in green paint. Add thick black eyeliner around the eyes, black lipstick, and don't leave home without a wart or three (see page 23). Black fingernails—contrasting gruesomely with green hands—are a witch's manicure of choice. For your witchly 'do, we recommend making your hair stringy with gel or ratting it with a brush and hairspray, and then throwing in some cobwebs and plastic spiders. You'll need to buy that pointy black hat that no self-respecting witch is ever without. Make sure you have your ride: a straw, wooden-handled broom.

- A cuter **teen witch** might wear the same hat, a black miniskirt, green and black striped tights, and pointy black shoes.

- Or drip glue onto your traditional black witch's hat and cape, and pour sand on them: let it all dry and you're a **sand witch.**

- To go the **good witch** route, wear a white, pink, or pastel dress or skirt—as puffy as possible. Dust yourself with glitter. Carry a glittery magic wand and wear a white witch's hat (if you can't find one, you can cover a black witch's hat with white duct tape and glue stars and glitter to it). Carry a basket of flower petals or pixie dust.

Witches, Both Wicked and Wonderful

A woman wearing a black robe and a pointy hat flies on a broomstick across the night sky. Her skin is green and warty, her hair ratty. For a moment, she hovers silhouetted against the full moon with a black cat perched demurely behind her. Then suddenly, she nosedives toward earth and lets out a bloodcurdling cackle.

If this isn't a classic Halloween image, what is? Terrorizing children, muttering evil spells over boiling cauldrons, and flaunting their aerodynamic brooms, these wild women have, well, bewitched our imaginations for ages.

Of course, not all witches want to "get you and your little dog, too!" Good witches use their magical powers to fight their uglier and grumpier sisters. There's glittering Glinda, the Good Witch of the East in *The Wizard of Oz* and the beautiful and (usually) sweet witches from *Bewitched; Sabrina, the Teenage Witch;* and *Charmed.* J. K. Rowling's books, starring Harry Potter, depict a whole world of witches and wizards dedicated to using their magical powers for good (and others, alas, who use them for evil). Or check out Gregory Maguire's inventive play, *Wicked,* on Broadway.

Glinda the Good Witch is blond and beloved.

Sabrina and her talking kitty.

Calling all flying monkeys!

How to Make a Wart from Scratch

Listen up, my pretty . . . You can't possibly leave the house as the Wicked Witch of the West without a truly disgusting wart on your chin. First, pop off the eraser from a pencil. Then cut a few bristles from your hairbrush and stick them inside the eraser like a pincushion. Glue the eraser to your desired wart location using spirit gum. Wait until dry, and then paint over your hairy wart with the color you're using on the rest of your face.

Let your inner witch come out to play.

The Salem Witch Trials of 1692

In the fourth century, the Christian Church officially denounced witchcraft and its worshiping of pagan deities, leading to the eventual persecution of anyone believed to be a witch or wizard. For hundreds of years, thousands of innocent men and women were tortured and killed in an effort to eradicate witchcraft. The 1692 witch trials in Salem, Massachusetts are perhaps the most famous example of these horrific events.

For the past 300 years, scholars have tried to understand the underlying causes of the Salem Witch Trials. The answer lies within a combination of economic, social, and religious concerns unique to life in the seventeenth century Massachusetts Bay Colony. A constant fear of attack by warring Indian tribes in the region, the revocation of the Massachusetts Bay Colony charter by Charles II, a firm belief in the devil, and a politically divided township created the oil onto which the lit match of the first witch accusations was flung.

In January of 1692, Reverend Samuel Parris of Salem Village called in Dr. William Griggs to treat the sudden illnesses of his nine-year-old daughter, Betty, and his twelve-year-old niece, Abigail Williams, who lived and worked with the Reverend's family after her own parents died. Unable to trace the girls' strange behavior to any physical ailment, Dr. Griggs made what would prove to be a far more fatal diagnosis: bewitchment.

Witchcraft, in those days, was directly linked to the Devil—it was believed that witches sold their souls to the "Black Man" in exchange for supernatural powers, with which they could invoke their own evil. The highly superstitious Puritans in Salem read their hardships as God's punishment for harboring these agents of the devil.

Almost immediately, names and accusations were "cried out" by the tormented, confused girls. As one scholar notes, those first accused fit a convenient profile: the socially marginal. The accusations escalated quickly; eventually, over 150 people were crammed in prison. Of those interned, nineteen were hanged, one was pressed to death, and as many as thirteen died in jail.

Playwright Arthur Miller examined the Salem Witch Trials—the social phenomenon and the consequences of mass hysteria—in *The Crucible*. He wrote the play as a response to the Red scare and McCarthyism of the 1950s, a period of paranoia and persecution reminiscent of the events of the 1690s.

CHAPTER TWO

SHOOTING STAR
page 43

Play with Your Words

Want to win cleverest costume this year? Want to impress that special someone with your creativity? Here are a few surefire contenders.

HOT DOG
page 35

QUEEN BEE
page 42

WEB SURFER
page 46

A SALT AND BATTERY

For Mr. and Miss Demeanor. One of you dresses up as a life-size **battery.** This involves designing a large piece of poster board to look like a battery—copy one you have in the house or make one up, maybe including a lightning bolt logo and the battery size (AA, D, etc.). Don't forget to put a plus sign on one end and a minus sign on the other. The other person dresses up as a **salt shaker.** The primary elements of this outfit are a cylinder (see box, right) made out of white poster board and a colander to wear on your head. Alternatively, you could be a salt container, which is simply a cylinder—model yourself after your favorite brand! (A variation from our pal Lindley and her friend, who spiced up Halloween one year by dressing as **salt and pepper shakers**—in white and black boxes and matching bowls covered with aluminum foil on their heads.)

Wearable Cylinders

To make a cylinder that you can wear you'll need a piece of poster board large enough to fit around your body with a bit of extra room, five or six brass fasteners or clear packing tape, and some string. Start by using a pencil to sketch the desired design, then paint or use markers to fill it in. When you're satisfied with your artwork, use a hole punch to make five or six holes down one side of what will be the seam. Line it up with the other side of the seam so that the edge with the holes overlaps the other side a bit. Use a pencil to mark where you'll need to put holes in the other side of the seam, and then use the hole punch to make the holes. Make two holes in the front and two in the back at the top of your cylinder, and thread a piece of string through them to put over your shoulders so the cylinder comes up to your armpits. Now put your arms into the string, hold the poster board closed, and—if you think you might use your cylinder again—fasten (or have a friend fasten) the seam together with the brass fasteners. If your creation is destined for the garbage can at the end of the night, tape the seam with clear packing tape.

BLACK-EYED PEA & BLACK-EYED SUSAN

Here are two easy ones. A **black-eyed pea** wears all white or tan, a big *P* written on or pinned to her shirt, and dark makeup around one eye. A **black-eyed Susan** has the same dark circle around one eye. She wears all yellow and sports a "Hello: My name is Susan" name tag.

BLIND DATE

Cut four holes just the right size for your legs and arms in a large brown trash bag. Fill it halfway with crumpled newsprint paper (available at craft stores—real newspaper would leave your clothes a smeary mess). Step inside, draw the top together around your neck and have a friend tape the bag shut with brown duct tape. Wear dark sunglasses and use a white cane (a piece of ½-inch dowel about 4 feet long, painted white with a red tip will do the trick).

Bruises, Scrapes, Cuts, and Scars

Bruises can make you look tougher, wimpier, or more decomposed. Don't worry; we've not suggesting you beat yourself up in the name of a better costume. Use red, yellow, purple, black, and even green face makeup for your desired effect. Apply your first color (probably black, purple, or red) with a makeup sponge. Try to avoid perfect circles or straight lines as irregular shapes look more realistic. After you have applied the first layer, add different colors over and around it until you've got a realistic-looking shiner. Blend the colors well. Remember that bruises fade into lighter colors toward their outer edges.

To create **scrapes** on your skin, use fake blood applied with the end of a tongue depressor. Dip the tongue depressor into the fake blood and drag it lightly across your skin in slightly crooked lines. If you use less blood and make smaller lines, the scrapes will be more believable.

If you've never seen a **fake cut** up close, you might be surprised by how ghastly a gash can look. If you want to make people wonder whether you've just fallen through a window, you can either buy a latex flesh wound at the store or create your own with putty. If you choose to create your own, rub the flesh-colored putty in your palms to warm it up. Apply it to your skin in a lump with the edges smoothed into your skin. Use a tongue depressor to create a ridge in the putty and then to fill it with fake blood. Allow a little trickle of the fake blood to pour out of the cut.

Scars are a little more difficult. You can try one freehand with face makeup—try a color a few shades lighter than your own—but it will be hard to make it look authentic. If you want realistic scars we recommend you buy a product called Rigid Collodion (a quarter-ounce bottle is about $4). It's a clear solution that wrinkles your skin as it dries, and it can be removed simply by peeling it off. You should be able to find Rigid Collodion at any decent costume shop or online.

THE BLIND LEADING THE BLIND

Another good one (of questionable taste): You and a friend both need dark sunglasses, white canes (see page 27), and fake bruises and cuts.

BLOOMIN' IDIOT

Every village has one—an idiot, that is. To look the part, we suggest a beanie, a short-sleeve button-down shirt tucked into your pants at chest level, and goofy fake teeth (or blacken out a few—see page 226). To step it up a notch, cover yourself in flowering vines, readily available at any craft or dollar store. Paint flowers on your face and attach a few flowers to your clothing. Your friends can't figure out what you're supposed to be? Then it's possible that *they* are the **bloomin' idiots**. Hey, better than a bloody one— for that, pour fake blood (see page 16) all over your costume. Don't forget to use your best British accent.

CANDLE IN THE WIND

Dress all in white. Glue yellow and red poster board "flames"—shaped as though they're being blown to one side—to a headband. If you want, carry a blown-out umbrella and safety-pin a piece of newspaper to one side of your body to emphasize the windiness.

CATCH-22

Damned if you do, damned if you don't? If you're so caught up in a dilemma that you haven't had time to think about what to wear to the party that's a mere fifteen minutes away, we can recommend a costume. Cut two large number twos out of construction paper or felt, and pin them to the front of your shirt ("22"). Drape a large net (available at sporting goods stores) over your head and shoulders.

CEREAL KILLER

You've got ten bucks in your pocket and twenty minutes (or less) to get into costume. Don't despair! Take a quick trip to your local drugstore and pick up a box of plastic knives and two packs of miniature cereal boxes. Stab the plastic knives into the boxes (you may have to cut or break off the tips to make them stick in); then pin the boxes to your clothing. There's a **cereal killer** on the loose!

CHEST OF DRAWERS

Looking for something quick and easy? To become a chest of drawers, simply pin a couple of pairs of boxers or panties to your chest.

CHICK MAGNET

Are women irresistibly drawn to you? Then you must be a **chick magnet.** This costume is very easy: Simply pin, staple, or glue baby chicks (the fuzzy kind found in novelty shops or, if you're the pack-rat type, marshmallow chicks leftover from Easter) to your all-black clothing.

DAIRY QUEEN

Hail to the Queen! Wear a white dress, with a white "regal" wrap (cow print, perhaps?) draped on top. Find a tiara or a crown and top off your "scepter" (any ½-inch dowel spray painted to match your crown will do) with a hunk of cheese. Carry a bottle of milk for refreshment. Get creative and make some dairy accessories—a "chain" belt of mini-cheeses strung together perhaps? Or affix mini plastic cows to your tiara and earrings. And a Laughing Cow cheese wedge can make a lovely pendant.

DEAD MAN WALKING

There are working stiffs, and then there are walking stiffs . . . Dress yourself as a gruesome corpse (ripped, dirty clothing; white, pasty, greenish skin on your face and hands; dark circles around your eyes; a zombie expression), and hit the party as a **dead man walking.**

DIRTY LAUNDRY

Here's an easy one to sort out. Cut a hole in a plastic laundry basket large enough for you to step into and pull up to your waist. Attach a pair of suspenders to the top edge, and wear it around your belly. Then, overfill the basket with laundry (old socks, T-shirts, etc.), an empty bottle of detergent (lighter than a full bottle), and dryer sheets. Who said you shouldn't air your **dirty laundry** in public? (Tip: If you can find one of those "hip-hugging" laundry baskets that molds to your body, you can belt it on and avoid the cutting.)

FREUDIAN SLIP

Tap into your subconscious as a **Freudian slip** this Halloween. Give a cheap full-length slip a little therapy: Use markers to write "id," "ego," and "superego" on the front; in the center of your back, write the famous definition: "When you say one thing and mean your mother." Around it, write classic Freudian slips, like "She's my breast friend," and "This isn't an erection— I mean, rejection."

"Did I really just say that?"

GOLD DIGGER

Dress all in gold, and carry a shovel with the tip painted gold. If you're going with a guy, get him to dress as a wealthy-looking geriatric (blue blazer, ascot, monopoly money coming out of his pockets).

"Looking for a date, grandpa?"

Age in an Instant

Apply your thickest foundation or pancake makeup—preferably in a tone that's slightly paler than your natural skin tone. Now scrunch up every muscle in your face and hold for a few breaths. When you release, all of your wrinkle lines should be visible. Yikes! Emphasize these lines by tracing them lightly with brown eyeliner. Create crow's-feet around your eyes. Apply brown shadow underneath your cheekbones and eyes. To get gray hair, sprinkle it with baby powder, use spray-in color, or brush in some white greasepaint.

HEAD IN THE CLOUDS

Who doesn't space out from time to time, daydreaming about sipping wine in a villa in Tuscany . . . while sitting in a cubicle drinking stale coffee from a vending machine? (Well, some of us do it more than others.) For those who hover at 30,000 feet most of the time: Wear sky-blue clothing and cover your upper body and shoulders in piles of cotton balls, gauze, scrunched up tissues, or anything else that resembles cumulus. Cover a hood or hat in more cotton so it looks like you have your **head in the clouds.**

HIGH AS A KITE

Here's another super-easy costume. Carry a ready-made kite. When people ask what you are, hold the kite up next to your head and in your best stoner voice, tell them you're **high as a kite,** man.

HOT DOG

See Spot . . . pant? Dress up as a puppy (brown clothes and makeup, floppy ears made with brown felt glued to a felt headband, tail, and collar) and add a Chinese fan to cool yourself. Who's in the mood for a **hot dog?**

IN ADVERTISING

Clip advertisements from magazines and newspapers and pin them to your clothing. When anyone asks, let them know you're **in advertising.**

INDIGO GIRLS

For two gals: Invest in or concoct a large quantity of light purple body paint and wear all periwinkle and violet. Step out as the **Indigo Girls.** No guitars required.

KILLING TIME

Make an enormous clock face out of cardboard. Cut a slit and stab a plastic dagger through it. Punch a hole at two o'clock and ten o'clock and thread a ribbon through them, and tie the clock around your neck. Affect a nonchalant, "I've got nowhere to be" expression.

LOVE BUG

Dress in shades of red and pink. Draw big red hearts on both cheeks and sew a bigger pink heart to your red shirt (or a red heart to your pink shirt). Don insect antennae and wings (see page 5). Give a few harmless nibbles during the night: Who wouldn't mind being bitten by the **love bug?**

MISGUIDED YOUTH

Ah, kids today. Here's how to get the look of a **misguided youth:** Find a beanie with a spinner on it, a backpack or campy lunch box, overalls, and an oversized lollipop. Bring a few maps, folded out and crumpled up in both hands to give the appearance that you're completely, hopelessly lost—and the maps have been useless. A broken compass is another good prop.

Freshman disorientation

MISTER OR MISS SMARTY-PANTS

Think you have all the answers? Glue those little, sour smartie candies all over your pants, and you really are **Mister** or **Miss Smarty-Pants!**

NICE GUY FINISHING LAST

Have a silver marathon cape in your closet? Wear your best "nice guy" outfit (jeans and dark shirt or khaki pants and dress white shirt) and tape a high number on your back. Wear your cape, carry Gatorade, and pin a black ribbon to your chest with the word *Last.* (Pin a round piece of paper to one end of two 5-inch pieces of ribbon.) Be your usual charming self, passing out lollipops and compliments, and you're a **nice guy finishing last.**

Mix up your props if you like. This "nice guy" is carrying groceries. That's nice.

LAST
NICE GUY
MARATHON PARTICIPANT

NO-BRAINER

Don a hospital gown, slippers, and a medical identification bracelet, and wrap your head in gauze bandages with some drops of red on your forehead. Carry a jar filled with part (or even better, all) of a head of cauliflower. No one will be surprised if you can't remember what you're supposed to be. You are, after all, a **no-brainer.**

ONE-NIGHT STAND

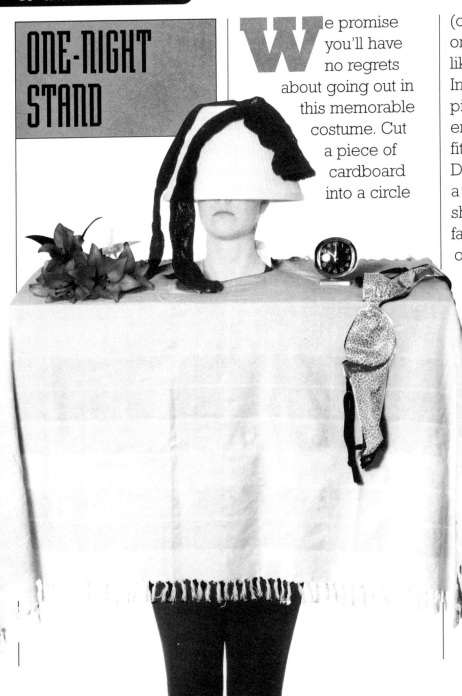

We promise you'll have no regrets about going out in this memorable costume. Cut a piece of cardboard into a circle (or a square, depending on what shape you'd like your table to be). In the middle of that piece cut a circle wide enough for your head to fit comfortably through. Drape the board with a lace or simple white sheet, and staple the fabric in place so it hangs over the edges. Cut around the hole for your head, so that the hole is still open. Next, glue on a small alarm clock, a bra or a stretched out pair of fishnets, and a book (glue these to cover the staples). Add an open matchbook with a number scribbled inside. As the finishing touch, wear a large lampshade as a hat (tie it in place with two pieces of ribbon).

POINTLESS

Wear all black. Use clear packing tape to attach unsharpened pencils all over your clothing. Say meaningless things all night.

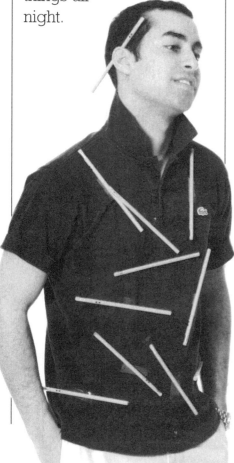

POTHEAD

Everyone has a pot, right? Then everyone can be a **pothead**—by sticking it on their heads like a baseball cap. Add your favorite hippie shirt and carry plenty of junk food for the munchies. Don't worry—it's legal.

QUEEN BEE

Your metamorphosis into a **queen bee** will require a little handiwork. (See if you can find a worker bee to do it for you!) First, make or buy a pair of black wings (see page 5). Then work on your outfit. You'll need to put on a black leotard or T-shirt, black leggings or shorts, and black tights. Use yellow duct tape to make stripes all across your torso. For the crowning touch: Buy a golden tiara and attach two black pipe cleaners as antennae. Carry a black and yellow striped scepter.

Note: a small variation on the costume—a black body and orange and black wings—and you've metamorphosed into a **monarch butterfly.**

ROLL IN THE HAY

Pick yourself a bale of hay (even urbanites can find hay fairly easily at markets and florists with seasonal offerings on display). Wear both a long-sleeved T-shirt and a button-down shirt with a pocket. Stuff handfuls of the hay between your shirts and in your pocket so that some of it is sticking out of your sleeves, waist, etc. Get some hay stuck in your hair, too. Stick a small, store-bought bread roll into your shirt pocket. What beats a good **roll in the hay?**

I'm almost too sexy.

SELF-ABSORBED

"**E**nough about me, let's talk about you," quips Bette Midler's character in *Beaches*. "So what do you think of me?" To become **self-absorbed,** pin sponges all over your clothing. A hand mirror is a good added prop.

SHOOTING STAR

Don't you know that you are a **shooting star?** Others will, if you cut two large stars out of yellow poster board and suspend them over your shoulders like a sandwich board (see page 174). Optional: Decorate them with a lot of glitter. Carry a brightly colored plastic water gun in each hand.

SOCIAL CLIMBER

Here's the perfect costume to validate your packrat ways. What other costume allows you to combine your black-tie best with the musty hiking equipment you stash away for 364 days of the year?

Step 1: Excavate old hiking shorts, boots, thick wool socks, carabiners, a compass, climbing pick, canteen, coils of rope, or any other accoutrements of camping that you might have crammed under the bed. Dirt adds authenticity. Add a scrape or cut to a knee (see page 28).

Step 2: Now get the top half of your body all gussied up. Women, wear a sequined halter top (or something equally fancy), add pearls and your biggest, flashiest costume jewelry. Men, go for either a tux jacket and bow tie, or dinner jacket and ascot. And ladies, don't leave home without your helmet-hair (two cans of Aquanet, or spray starch in a pinch). What you end up with is a strikingly mismatched outfit—the top half, formal and fancy; the bottom half, ready to hike.

Finally, as you mingle at the party—air-kissing all your chums and having a too, too fabulous time—you might choose to remember that the canteen is a close cousin of the flask. Why do you think campers are so notoriously happy?

STIR-CRAZY

Here's an easy one to whip up, terrible pun intended. Buy a box of stir sticks and tape them all over your clothing. Add whisks, an egg beater, wooden spoons . . . you've gone **stir-crazy.**

TROPHY WIFE

Find out what it's like to be permanent arm candy. Put on your sexiest cocktail dress, wear classy makeup, sport an enormous glittery engagement ring, and carry a trophy.

Anti-Costume Antics

Know someone who *hates* dressing up for Halloween? A Halloween Scrooge who says, "Bah humbug" instead of "Trick-or-Treat?" Try recommending the following **low-budget, low-enthusiasm costumes:**

1. Time Traveler from the Day Before Halloween
2. Alien Disguised as Human
3. Yourself in a Sweater You Don't Usually Wear
4. Depressed Person Acting Cheerful
5. Depressed Person No Longer Acting Cheerful

WEB SURFER

Totally cyber, dude . . . Dress like a surfer (board shorts, zinc oxide on your nose, shades, flip-flops). Drape yourself with some of that fake spiderweb stuff you can find at any drugstore or Halloween store in October, and you're a **Web surfer.**

WHITE TRASH

Wear all white. Crumple up white tissues, clean milk and egg cartons (the whiter the better), and white loose-leaf paper, and staple or safety-pin them all over your clothing.

CHAPTER THREE

BATHING BEAUTY
page 48

FRENCH MAID
page 58

WONDER WOMAN
page 67

Come-Hither Costumes

Halloween presents a perfect opportunity to show off your sexy, glamorous side. That doesn't mean baring all (although it could)—it just means tapping into the right costume to really turn up the heat. The following getups are guaranteed to sizzle.

BATHING BEAUTY

If you've got a bubbly personality, attach small white balloons all over a skin-colored bodysuit (use safety pins below the knot of the balloon). Wear high heels, glamorous fake eyelashes, and lots of makeup. Don a bathing cap and carry a back scrubber or a yellow Rubber Duckie.

BELLY DANCER

What's more alluring than a sensuous dancer? Billowing pants, finger cymbals, a shirt tied above your navel, and maybe a wrap draped over your head and face for dramatic effect. String a gold chain with charms around your waist, and wear as much jewelry on your wrists and ankles as you can find. Now shimmy! (As a variation, carry an ornate bottle, put your hair up in a high ponytail, and you're a **genie,** recently let out of your bottle.)

Batting an Eye: False Eyelashes

What do Daisy Buchanan, Betty Boop, Diana Ross, and Tammy Faye Baker all have in common? Well, not much, actually—but Halloween revelers intending to dress up as these ladies can all wear a common accessory: false eyelashes. You *could* thicken your lashes with eight coats of mascara, but it just can't compare to the fun and glamor of batting thick, luxurious falsies.

There are two options if you want to go the false route. Individual false lashes applied near the outer corners of the eyes look more natural, but they require a steady hand and

a bit of practice. We're all for the natural look—most of the year. On Halloween, though, we want to be stunning, dramatic, drop-dead gorgeous! That means using full false eyelashes.

Before you begin, hold the lashes up to your eye. If the band is too long, trim it. Smudge some dark eyeliner right above your lash line to help hide the band. Dip your finger in the adhesive that comes with the false lashes. After 30 seconds, when the glue has become tacky,

BETTY BOOP

carefully drag the lash band through it. Attach the lashes just above your lash line, and as close to it as possible. Gently press the lashes down until they adhere. Finally, curl your new and old lashes together, and apply a couple of coats of mascara.

To remote: The lashes will come off more easily if you rub them with eye makeup remover to soften the adhesive first.

As glamorous as you'll feel, and as fun as false eyelashes are, save them for special occasions. Even though the adhesive is made for the delicate skin of your eyelids, it can still cause irritation.

CABANA BOY OR GIRL

Throw on your tightest, smallest white shorts, a white polo shirt, white tennis shoes, and a towel over your shoulders. A fruity drink (with umbrella) in one hand, a bottle of Hawaiian Sun in the other, and you're the resort's favorite **cabana boy** or **girl.** (Replace the props with a tennis racket and a white visor, and you're a **tennis pro.**)

CAMERAMAN FOR "GIRLS GONE WILD"

Hey, fellas, you're sure to see some action in this costume. All you need is a video camera with the name of the show prominently displayed, a T-shirt from Cancun (for example), Mardi Gras beads to wear and give away, and a handful of photo release forms.

CAR MECHANIC

No one can resist a guy who can fix things. Find a one-piece work suit (any hardware megastore will have it in stock, or find one at a used-clothing store). Write your name in cursive and "Bob's Auto Shop" in block letters on the left breast of your suit. Add some dark stains to the front of your suit, and have an old rag and a wrench sticking out of your back pocket.

CATWOMAN

This is the *purr*fect costume for the girl who wants to be a sex kitten this Halloween. Dress in black (vinyl or leather is best)—a tight top and tight pants or a very short skirt—and find some black stiletto boots to give yourself that long, feline look. Should you be able to muster up the courage to go in and buy (let alone wear) a pair of thigh-high patent leather boots, they'd be ideal. You also need long fake nails, a whip, and a pair of black cat ears. A cat mask that covers your eyes is optional. *Meow.* For a twosome, combine with **Batman** (a costume that may be worth renting)—a dark gray bodysuit (or the closest thing you've got), with black gloves, black boots, a black cape, a yellow utility belt, and a black half-face mask with tiny felt ears attached. Lastly, make sure that famous bat emblem is emblazened on the chest.

CHIPPENDALE'S DANCER

Strut your stuff! Black leather pants, a bow tie, and some dollar bills emerging from your waistband are all you need. Keep in mind that you don't have to have rock-solid abs to get into this costume—remember Chris Farley's *Saturday Night Live* Chippendale dancer?

COUPLE CAUGHT ON LOVERS' LANE

Maybe you and your lovebug have let your Halloween costume planning take a backseat this year. So follow suit! Get some of that backseat action yourselves, and emerge as a **couple caught on Lovers' Lane.** Girls: bird-nesty hair (to "rat" your hair, run a comb from the ends of your hair up to your scalp, instead of from the scalp down), skirt tucked into the undies, misbuttoned blouse, smudged makeup. Then double-load the lipstick and leave kiss marks all over your guy—on every visible inch of skin. Good props for guys: Binaca, a pair of nylon panty hose or panties pinned to a pant leg (in a way that looks like static cling), messy hair, loosened tie, and unbuttoned shirt.

But don't just play this one by our book—coming up with your own *in flagrante* inspiration is much more fun.

DANCERS FROM MOULIN ROUGE

Sex appeal for a group! Throw on your fishnets, garter belts, your sexiest camisoles, and short shorts; your pearls, your feathers, big hair, bigger heels, lots of dramatic makeup (rouge circles, moles, smoky eyes), and—if you can find them—those can-can skirts, short in the front with layers of petticoats. Get ready to strut your stuff!

Can you can-can?

DAISY DUKE

Weather permitting (we'd hate to be responsible for anyone's case of frostbite or hypothermia), **Daisy Duke** from the *Dukes of Hazard* is a costume you won't hear any complaints about. Her signature item of clothing, of course, is itty-bitty, teeny-weeny cut-off shorts. If you've got what it takes, we say put on your sheer panty hose and high heels and go for it. But the exhibitionism doesn't end there. Tie your gingham button-down shirt in a knot high on your stomach, and keep it buttoned low enough to show maximum cleavage. Tuck a miniature Confederate flag in your back pocket, fluff your hair into a big, wavy mane, and chew suggestively on a long piece of hay.

DIRK DIGGLER

For your **Dirk Diggler** costume, up your endowment (hey, no shame in using balled-up socks) and cut loose in flashy, fabulous *Boogie Nights* gear. Break out that gold playboy medallion, the butterfly-collared polyester suit, and the rainbow-colored platform shoes you've been storing since 1976.

FARMER'S DAUGHTER

Aw, shucks—is it October 30 and little ol' you don't have a costume yet? Why not go as a **farmer's daughter?** Take a flannel or gingham shirt and tie it in a knot above your waist. A denim skirt or jeans and cowboy boots are the perfect complements. Pleat hair into two braids or pigtails, and tie each with a gingham ribbon. A smattering of freckles across the nose and cheeks can be drawn on with brown eyeliner pencil. Add a missing tooth if you want to tone down the sex appeal. A straw cowboy-style hat completes the look.

FLASHER

Do friends often complain, "My dear, we don't see *enough* of you"? Here's a way to redeem yourself. Underneath a belted trenchcoat, put on your sexiest skivvies—or a flesh-colored body suit—and flash the crowd at intervals. (Clearly not a costume for the weak of heart.)

Halloween Home Decor

Whether you're planning to host a Halloween bash or not, sprucing up your home for the holiday is a great way to get into the spirit of the season. Before you begin, take a good look at the space you're decorating and brainstorm its possible transformations. There are lots of simple things you can do—like winding plastic snakes around the banister, hanging bats off the chandeliers, spreading cobwebs on the bookshelves, or sitting a mummy on the couch. (By the way, it doesn't have to cost a fortune to redecorate your residence. Think about the things you already have lying around, like old sheets and floodlights, and put them to good use.)

FOR THE PORCH AND FRONT YARD

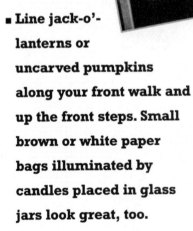

- **Line jack-o'-lanterns or uncarved pumpkins along your front walk and up the front steps. Small brown or white paper bags illuminated by candles placed in glass jars look great, too.**

- **Make gravestones out of plywood (or cardboard if you're going to keep them on the porch). Paint them gray and write funny epitaphs on them. Cover them with cotton cobwebs and prop them around your yard. Point floodlights on them at night, and for an extra spooky effect, place a fake arm coming out of the ground in front of one of them.**

- **Hang ghosts made out of sheets from the porch ceiling and trees.**

- **Point floodlights into trees to create ghostly shadows.**

- Play eerie music from a stereo propped in a window.

INSIDE THE HOUSE

- Dim the lighting. Your den needs to be dark and dank. Either turn off the lights and use candles or low-lit lamps, or cover lampshades with dark cellophane paper. (Be careful to avoid any direct contact with bulbs—a definite fire hazard.)

- Create a centerpiece on your dining room table or fireplace mantle with pumpkins, autumn leaves, and cotton cobwebs. Or float tiny pumpkins (the ones that easily fit in the palm of your hand) and floating candles in bowls of water. Use clear glass bowls and dye the water green or black with food coloring.

- Cut bats from construction paper and hang them with thread from the ceiling, chandeliers, and doorways.

- Haunt your house by stuffing a mummy, Grim Reaper, scarecrow, or one of each, and propping them up around the house.

- Cut out silhouettes of ghosts, bats, witches, and black cats in the classic Halloween pose from large pieces of paper and use painter's tape to affix them to the walls and windows. Small bat silhouettes can be taped to the insides of lampshades.

- Fill a large pot or cauldron with dry ice and let it "bubble and boil" all night in the corner. (But don't let anyone touch the ice.)

- For the finishing touch, visit your local toy store or dollar store, and buy inexpensive plastic rats, lizards, hands, and other creepy objects. Litter your house with these little beasts, and place them strategically for a startling effect. Cover the last few undecorated areas with cotton cobwebs and sprinkle them with plastic spiders.

FLIGHT ATTENDANT

Nothing said sexy in the seventies like a **flight attendant:** the blue eye shadow, the stiffly sprayed winged hair à la Farrah Fawcett, the tight-fitting polyester uniforms. The basic getup is simple: pumps, nude panty hose, fitted blue blazer, short scarf jauntily tied at the neck, tan or blue skirt to just above the knee, and white shirt with a Peter Pan collar. Design some air safety cards. Dig around to see if you can find the flight wings pin from your first-ever plane ride. Otherwise, cut one out of cardboard and paint it silver. Pass out peanuts and be friendlier and more patient that you've ever been before. Your costume is guaranteed to take off.

FRENCH MAID

And speaking of *amour* . . . only a French gal could take an outfit designed for housework and chores, and turn it into one of the most popular male fantasies. We're talking about the classic **French maid's** costume, which falls squarely in the category of "how to have sex appeal without really trying." Wear a low-cut little black dress with a short, flared skirt. (A tight black shirt and short skirt will also do.) Add fishnets or sheer stockings with seams, black stilettos, a feather duster, a ruffled lace headpiece, and that trademark little white apron. (You might have to buy the last two items, available at any Halloween shop.) Don't be surprised if things get a little dirty.

GOD'S GIFT TO WOMEN

Think this describes you perfectly? Then there's only one costume for you, Stud. Wrap a large box like an enormous present and tie it up with red ribbon with a bow facing front. Cut holes for your head, arms, and torso. Attach a large poster board gift tag, on which you've written in large letters:

To: WOMEN
FROM: GOD

Unless this is too subtle.

LADY GODIVA

An homage to our favorite purveyor of chocolate, and a great costume for someone who likes to make an entrance. The most obvious ingredient is the very, very long, thick, blond wig—you'll probably have to hit a Halloween store for that.

Then you'll need a flesh-colored bodysuit and nude panty hose. Pin your blonde mane to the bodysuit in the places a bathing suit would cover. Go barefoot indoors and wear simple sandals when you're out. (The white horse, unless you're Bianca Jagger, might be a feat to pull off.) If you're feeling generous, hand out chocolate truffles.

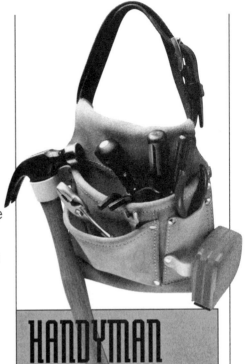

HANDYMAN

Throw on your overalls, flannel shirt, construction boots, strap on a tool belt, and you're a **handyman** to have around. Ladies, for a female version, think Pamela Anderson as the Tool Time Girl in *Home Improvement*—same basics (but tighter clothing), delivered with sex appeal.

HUGH HEFNER

Here's one for the guy who fancies himself a ladies' man, and has a gaggle of girls willing to tag along. Go as the quintessential bachelor, **Hugh Hefner,** with the trademark red velvet smoking jacket, salt-and-pepper hair, pipe, copy of *Playboy,* and bottle of Viagra peeking out of your chest pocket. As for the bevy of blond **Bunnies** flanking you on every side, advise them that less is more in the clothing department. Except when it comes to the wonders of the Wonderbra—in that one case, more is more. Bunnies should wear black lingerie or leotards with fluffy tails pinned to their rears, white wrist cuffs, white collars with black bow ties, fishnets, heels, and, of course, bunny ears.

HULA DANCER

Even if the weather outside is less than Caribbean, you can create some heat by showing up as a **hula dancer.** Pick up a coconut bra at a costume shop (though a bikini top will do, too), a grass skirt, and some brightly colored plastic leis to drape around your neck. (If you're feeling shy or if you'll be cold, don a flesh-colored shirt or bodysuit.) Wear flip-flops and a big fake flower in your hair. Dancing tip: Sway your hips gently back and forth, and move your arms in a similarly undulating pattern. Aloha!

HEIDI-HO

If you think the St. Pauli Girl has all the fun, here's your chance to join in. Don a dirndl and thigh-high white stockings. Braid your hair, and hoist a stein, and say *"Prost!"*

JAZZ SINGER

Ever dream of crooning "Stormy Weather" in a dimly lit nightclub for a crowd of adoring regulars? Even if you can't sing a note, your inner **Jazz Singer** can come out to play this Halloween. She'll need a sequined dress slit all the way up the thigh, big sparkly earrings, gloves up to the elbows, stiletto heels, shiny lipstick, and hair waved à la Billie Holiday or Josephine Baker. Don't forget a microphone and tip jar.

CLARK KENT/ SUPERMAN

Mild-mannered **Clark Kent** by day, **Superman** by night! Go as the conservatively downplayed *Daily Planet* ace reporter— you'll need thick, black-framed glasses, slicked hair, a suit, and a pencil tucked behind one ear. A blue T-shirt with the Superman logo underneath your shirt (undo a few buttons to give a sneak peak) reveals your alter ego to the citizens of Metropolis and fellow party-goers. Trail a few yellow pages from your shoe with double-sided tape, evidence of those lightning-fast changes in telephone booths. Have a budding love interest? Ask her to go as **Lois Lane,** the sexy

but buttoned-up reporter (gray business suit, notepad for jotting down scoops, and a demonstrable crush on "the man in the sky").

MATADOR

Olé! Going in a **matador** costume is sexy for a bullheaded type. Wear a black bolero, white shirt, black knickers, white knee-high socks, and black shoes, and slick your hair back. Wave a red cape in the air. The ladies will come charging.

CARMEN MIRANDA

Bring out your inner samba superstar. Get dolled up in your flashiest, shiniest, midriff-baring outfit, then go wild creating a tutti-frutti headdress—the more fruit, the merrier. Lots of gaudy costume jewelry completes the look.

SCHOOLGIRL

Exhibit A: A certain Britney Spears video. **Schoolgirls** can be sexy. *Exhibitionist* B: You. Borrow your sister's field hockey skirt, dig out your old Catholic school skirt, or buy any kilt-like skirt—as long as it's plaid. Tie a white button-down shirt in a knot above your navel, add some knee-high socks, saddle shoes, pigtails, and a little backpack. Extra props: a Lolita lollipop, an apple for the teacher, a pair of glasses. The naughtiness is all in the execution—we'll leave that up to you, dear reader. As a companion to the schoolgirl, the **naughty professor** loves private conferences and extra-credit assignments. Break out your most collegiate threads: corduroy blazer with patches over the elbows, sweater-vest, oxford shirt, tweed pants, boat shoes, tattered briefcase, glasses, *Playboy* in the back pocket.

SEXIEST MAN ALIVE

Design a large piece of poster board to look like the cover of *People* magazine's **"Sexiest Man Alive"** issue. (It doesn't have to be an exact replica. You just need to evoke the look with the words and maybe some pictures of a couple of "runners-up" glued to the top.) Cut out a space for your face to fit through, and you're this year's winner.

STRIPPER EMERGING FROM A CAKE

For the real exhibitionist, surprise everyone as a **stripper emerging from a cake.** Construct the two halves (you need to make a front and back) of the cake out of white poster board (use pink and green marker or strings of flowers to look like cake decorations). Punch two holes at the top of the front and back halves of the cake, and string them over your shoulders like suspenders. On your top half, all you need are a lace teddy or fancy bra and a boa. Your legs will be coming out of the bottom, so put on some fishnet stockings and high heels.

WONDER WOMAN

This year, recapture the campy, famously sexy appeal of Lynda Carter as **Wonder Woman**. There are a number of elements to this costume. Step 1. You'll need a red tube top and blue short shorts or miniskirt. Affix a bunch of white fabric iron-on stars to the shorts. Step 2. To make your crown and wrist cuffs, you'll need some gold fabric and a manila folder or two. Sketch a crown shape (don't forget the peak in front) on one folder, and then cut it out. Glue the gold material to it so the fold in the fabric covers the bottom of the crown. Do the same for the 3-inch-wide wrist cuffs (it doesn't matter which side the fold is on). Now put one red fabric iron-on star to the center of your crown and one to each wrist cuff. Step 3. If you don't have red boots, wear

a pair of black boots and pull a pair of thigh-high red stockings over them. Cut holes for the heels to fit through. Step 4. Wind a length of gold upholstery cord into a "lasso of truth" and hang it from a thick gold belt. Step 5. Finally, this costume demands dark hair, so if you're not naturally raven-haired, wear a wig or use a temporary hair dye.

Always a Bridesmaid?

What to do with your most hideous old bridesmaid dress? Turn it into a clever costume with one of the following ideas:

■ **Invisible Man's Date:**
Tired of going stag? Here's the easiest blind (deaf, dumb, and nonexistent) date you've ever faced. Throw on your bridesmaid gown and accessorize. On the waist (or bottom), pin a stuffed, outstretched, white glove to your outfit.

■ **Linda Evans as Crystal Carrington:**
You may need to add some shoulder pads to your poofy dress to make the look really authentic. And stock up on Aquanet—the '80s meant big hair (bonus points if yours is frosted). If you're not blond, you'll need a wig.

Add glittering fake jewels, pucker your lips and whine, "Oh, Blake!"

■ **Miss America:** Add a sash, easily made using a strip of white fabric with "Miss [name of your state]" written in black permanent marker. Wear white gloves and carry a bouquet of roses balanced in the crook of one arm. If you have friends on board, each of you should represent a different state. The winner wears a tiara. The losers have mascara streaks down their cheeks.

■ Poor **Carrie,** taunted and tormented by her classmates! Give the crowd chills as Stephen King's famously vengeful prom queen with telekinetic powers. Drench that hideous gown in fake blood—the ultimate revenge on a bad dress.

■ We've heard the horror stories: "The dress had magenta sequins with a sea-green sash, and a yellow flower embroidered on one of the poof sleeves" . . . "My hair was Nelly-Larsen-ringlets-go-to-the-1983-prom." Here's your chance to pull all those shudder-inducing tales of bridesmaid humiliation into one terrible look. Step into the dress and choose stockings and shoes, and possibly a wrap, in clashing colors. Pancake on the makeup, wage war on your hair, pick yourself a bouquet of weeds, and you're a **bridesmaid from hell:** Set the bar as low as it can go.

CHAPTER FOUR

1920s
FLAPPER
page 84

THOMAS
AQUINAS
page 70

QUEEN OF
ENGLAND
page 81

History in the Making

Look to the past for inspiration—you've got plenty of famous figures from which to choose. Make history this Halloween by going as the historical figure you find most intriguing (or simply the one you'd vote Best Dressed).

THOMAS AQUINAS

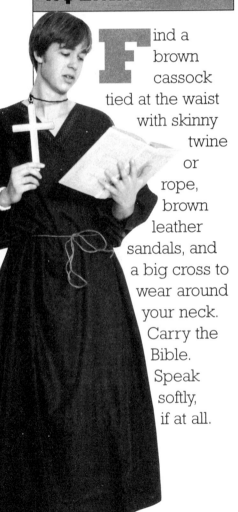

Find a brown cassock tied at the waist with skinny twine or rope, brown leather sandals, and a big cross to wear around your neck. Carry the Bible. Speak softly, if at all.

NEIL ARMSTRONG

"**T**hat's one small step for man, one giant leap for mankind." It's also—if we might add to **Neil Armstrong's** 1969 statement upon becoming the first person to walk on the moon— one terrific idea for a costume. Slip into white coveralls (available at hardware stores) and bulk up by padding them with newspaper. Affix a miniature American flag to your arm. Wear white snow boots (or cover your non-white snow boots with white thigh-high stockings, tucking any extra into the top of the boots). Add white ski gloves, and a white backpack—your oxygen tank. (If you don't happen to have a white backpack, cover a colored one with white duct tape.) Unfortunately, we've yet to come up with a smart and safe way of making a helmet— but it's a prop you'll find at any costume shop pre-season.

NAPOLEON BONAPARTE

"It's not the size of the dog in the fight, but the amount of fight in the dog," once claimed a very small terrier, before getting his collar handed to him in the first round by a German shepherd. The expression also applies to puny but powerful French emperor **Napoleon Bonaparte.** Whether or not you share his height complex, you can take a cue from his decked-to-the-gills military wardrobe this Halloween. You'll need a long blue coat with gold buttons and epaulets, white pants, tall black boots, a white shirt with a high lace collar, and a swashbuckling sword. And don't forget to strike his pose: a proud stance with your right hand tucked into your jacket.

GEORGE AND BARBARA BUSH

George wears a conservative suit with a red tie and glasses. His gray hair is parted to one side. **Barbara** stands out in a bright blue dress with three strands of pearls, a head of fluffy white hair, and she leads a brown and white English springer spaniel, Millie.

JULIUS CAESAR/NERO

All hail **Julius Caesar!** Make a delicate wreath (get vines—real or plastic —at a flower or craft shop) to rest upon your head, and don a toga (see **Goddess,** page 11) and leather sandals. Push all of your short hair forward onto your forehead. If you're part of a couple, pair up with **Cleopatra** (opposite). Carry a violin, and you're **Nero!**

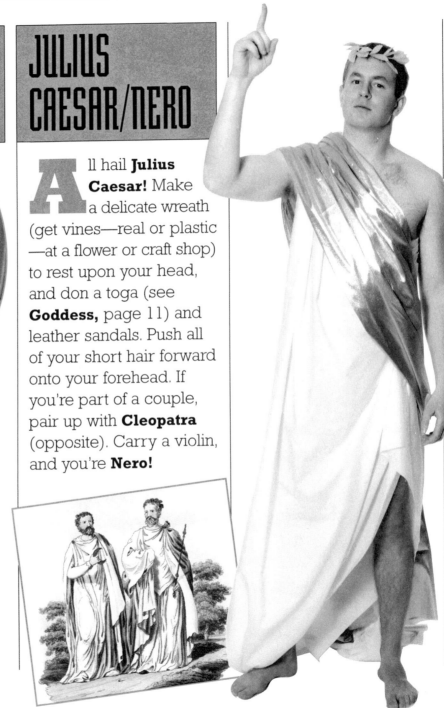

CHRISTOPHER COLUMBUS

Discover new territory as **Christopher Columbus.** You'll need a telescope, some old maps, knickers, a long velvet jacket, and a shirt with ruffles. Construct the steering wheel of your ship out of thick brown cardboard.

CLEOPATRA

Queen for a night! The Queen of the Nile was the reigning sex symbol of her time—not a bad act to follow. So ascend to your throne this Halloween and deck yourself out in an Egyptian headdress (a rich brocade fabric draped over your head and held in place with a thick gold cord), long royal robes or a toga in dark, dramatic colors, heavy black eye makeup, lace-up sandals, and a golden scepter. Add as much gold jewelry—armband, ear cuffs, bracelets—as you can find. Carry a

rubber asp. Dye your hair jet-black (make sure to use temporary dye). And last but not least, enlist a few good men to go as your entourage of shirtless male slaves. Get them to feed you grapes.

AMELIA EARHART/ CHARLES LINDBERGH/ THE WRIGHT BROTHERS

Here's a good way to get your wings. With a brown leather bomber jacket, white scarf, windblown hair, aviator goggles, jodhpurs, and a pilot's helmet, you've transformed yourself into **Amelia Earhart,** the first woman to fly solo across the Atlantic. Men, do the same and you're **Charles Lindbergh.** Or two buddies can go as the **Wright Brothers,** builders of the world's first airplane, by dressing up in brown three-piece suits and bowler hats, and carrying blueprints and model airplanes.

BENJAMIN FRANKLIN

Step out as one of our nation's founding fathers. This is a costume that works best if you have both male

pattern baldness and shoulder-length hair (add baby powder to give it the salt-and-pepper look). Don a ruffled white shirt, a long overcoat of either brown or blue, and small, circular, wire-rimmed glasses. If you don't have knickers (and who doesn't?), roll a pair of tan pants up to just below your knees, wear long white socks and brown shoes. Carry a copy of *Poor Richard's Almanack*.

MAHATMA GANDHI

Isn't it time to give peace a chance? Go as the ultimate pacifist this year. You'll need a bald cap, round-rimmed glasses, white flowing robe, a walking stick, and sandals. Decline hors d'oeuvres, or whatever food is served.

Hey, Baldie!

Worn properly, a bald cap can completely and dramatically change your appearance. Worn improperly, a bald cap can make you look ridiculous. Here is the right way.

First of all, make sure you have the right size bald cap for your head. If it's too big, your scalp will look weird and wrinkly. Brush your hair off your face and neck, and keep it off with lots of hairspray. Carefully pull the cap over your head, and ask someone to trim the "skin" around your ears. Tuck away any stray hairs. Apply adhesive (the bald cap will probably come with adhesive, but if it doesn't, make sure you buy some spirit gum) around the edges and make sure the cap is where you want it. Smooth down the edges so the cap blends in with your scalp. Wipe away any excess adhesive. If the cap doesn't look seamless, apply some foundation makeup to the edges.

MIKHAIL GORBACHEV

Wear a suit and add a wine-colored birthmark to your forehead. Carry around a bottle of vodka and pepper your conversations with words like *glasnost* and *perestroika*.

JOAN OF ARC

Play the martyr with a torn brown cassock or armor, a short boyish 'do, a huge cross around your neck, and a sword. Just *don't* play with matches.

ABRAHAM LINCOLN

All it takes to be honest **Abe Lincoln,** the sixteenth president of the United States, is a dark suit, black bow tie, white oxford shirt, short black beard, black top hat, and some of the Gettysburg address ("Fourscore and seven years ago . . ."). Being tall helps.

The Haunting of the White House

Who knew that 1600 Pennsylvania Avenue was located smack in the middle of the twilight zone? Turns out that the White House—home to every president and first lady since John and Abigail Adams—has been visited by many of its deceased former inhabitants.

Take **Abigail Adams,** for starters, who, after moving with the nation's capital from Philadelphia to Washington, D.C., found herself living in a poorly heated, damp White

House. She concluded that the East Room was the warmest and driest in which to hang her family's laundry to dry. Witnesses still see her ghost, wearing her lace cap and shawl, scurrying towards that room with her arms outstretched, as if carrying a large basket of wash.

Hot ticket **Dolley Madison,** wife of James, was charming, popular, feisty, and quick-tempered. During her time at the White House, one of her projects was to plan and build a beautiful Rose Garden. Apparently, it meant a lot to her, because when the second Mrs. Woodrow Wilson ordered the Rose Garden dug up, Dolley's ghost arrived at the scene to frighten off the workmen. Today, the Rose Garden remains just as Dolley planned it two centuries ago.

During his presidency, **Abe Lincoln** had premonitions of his own death. Ward Hill Lamon, a confidant of the President's, jotted down in 1865 that Lincoln told him he'd had several dreams in which he'd been assassinated. Many have reported sightings of Honest Abe within the White House walls. Some speculate that the traumatic nature of the end of his presidency has led him to linger—and to make himself visible to myriad presidents, first ladies, staff, and guests since his death in 1865.

IMELDA MARCOS

Craving some '80s excess? A bold-colored dress with butterfly sleeves; enormous dark hair; pancaked and overdone makeup and, of course, two tote bags brimming with shoes.

MARIE ANTOINETTE

Versailles is *always* in vogue as a Halloween pick. To capture the look of **Marie Antoinette,** mount your powder-white hair high on top of your head, with curled tendrils around your face. Raid a costume shop for a replica of an eighteenth-century dress (seriously low cut, tightly corseted, and richly brocaded), and deck yourself out with as much expensive-looking costume jewelry as possible. Lastly, you'll need a fake beauty mark and a plate with an enormous piece of cake (a reference to the queen's rumored response, "Let them eat cake!" when told that her subjects had no bread and were starving).

Big Wigs

For a total change of appearance, nothing beats a wig. A wig may be the one item that truly defines a look, whether it's a general look—a blond bombshell or a white-haired geriatric—or the look of a specific celebrity. Let's face it—if you want to look like George Washington, you *have* to have his 'do.

Wig prices vary widely. If you're planning to wear it only once, there's no reason to spend a fortune. Cheap acrylic wigs can cost as little as $25 and are available almost everywhere during the Halloween season at pharmacies and superstores like Target and Wal-Mart. The really good wigs are made out of high-quality synthetic materials or real human hair and can run as high as $1,500. They're available in wig salons and certain beauty parlors. You can also find a wide selection in costume shops and online.

If you have a full head of natural hair, either pull it back tightly and pin it close to your scalp, or buy a special cap designed to fit under your wig to tuck your hair into. (Spring for the cap if you're buying an expensive wig—it will protect it from scalp oils.) Use lots of bobby pins to secure your new head of hair, and remember to give your best shampoo-commercial head-tosses throughout the night.

MANUEL NORIEGA/ FIDEL CASTRO/ CHE GUEVARA

Green fatigues, red beret, machine gun, and a ball and chain around one ankle: You're former Panamanian dictator **Manuel Noriega.** For **Fidel Castro,** replace the beret and ball and chain with a cigar and a beard. Or go for radical **Che Guevara,** in a beret (with a star glued to the front), combat boots, and military gear.

ANNIE OAKLEY

Want to be a sartorial sharpshooter? No one shot sharper than wild Westerner **Annie Oakley.** Get your gun (brightly colored plastic, please), grab your hat, throw on that fringy leather vest, a flannel shirt, some dungarees, and cowboy boots. Yee haw!

EVA PERÓN

Argentina's most beloved and controversial first lady, **Eva Perón** has inspired a Broadway musical and a movie (starring Madonna, and worth seeing for inspiration) . . . so why not a Halloween costume? Her style was decadently haute couture: Christian Dior, furs, and a staggering collection of gems. For your purposes, go with a structured skirt suit with strong shoulder lines, a wasp waist, and a three-quarter-length skirt. Pull your hair back into a chignon. You'll also need a pillbox hat, seamed panty hose, and bright red lipstick. Hum "Don't Cry for Me, Argentina" under your breath.

POCAHONTAS

To embody **Pocahontas,** you'll need a mane of long black hair; a simple dress made of suede, light-colored leather, or tan or brown fabric; for your feet, Uggs, moccasins, or leather sandals; and a leather band around your head. Add turquoise and silver jewelry.

QUEEN OF ENGLAND

Mum's the word: Go as the **Queen of England** by graying your hair with baby powder and donning white gloves, a frumpy dress, and a pillbox hat. Or replace the hat with the fanciest tiara you can find and carry an ornate scepter in your left hand. With your right, wave to the crowds (keep your fingers together and your hand slightly cupped while turning your wrists slightly) as you pass by.

BETSY ROSS

To dress up as **Betsy Ross,** you'll need a floor-length black or calico dress, a white shawl, and a white bonnet. Carry a small sewing kit and a replica of the 1776 flag (with thirteen horizontal bands of alternating red and white, and thirteen white stars arranged in a circle on a blue background), which you've "just finished sewing."

GEORGE WASHINGTON

Command the crowds as the first president of the United States. Getting a head of hair like Washington's isn't easy—you'll probably have to buy a wig. Find or fake some turn-of-the-eighteenth-century garb (ideally, a blue coat with big brassy buttons, white knickers, tricorn hat, and tall black boots). Wear a white cotton scarf wrapped neatly around your neck with the ends falling down the front of your shirt. Carry a large rectangular piece of green poster board decorated as a one-dollar bill. Cut an oval out of the center, and pose with your mug in the space.

Ghosts Galore

Whether it's your grandmother, your best friend, or a neighbor, almost everyone knows someone who has seen a ghost during his or her lifetime. Maybe you've seen one yourself. Although cultural and religious beliefs vary, a common explanation is that these supernatural visitors are spirits of the dead stuck between this realm and the next, due to a traumatic or untimely death. Certain traditions are so universal among ghost stories that they can be classified. The most common kinds of ghost include:

- **Messenger ghosts: Shortly after death, these spirits return to our plane of existence—usually only once—to deliver messages to their loved ones. Messengers often bring words or feelings of comfort.**

- **Residual haunters: Residuals remain in the environment they inhabited during their lifetime. Howling house-haunters belong in this category.**

- **Poltergeists: These ghosts have the ability to affect the physical world. They slam doors, bang pipes, walk loudly overhead, flip light switches, even turn faucets on or off. And sometimes they do much worse. These mischief-makers generally star in the most hair-raising ghost stories.**

Q: What kind of streets do ghosts like best?

A: Dead ends.

The Decade-Inspired Theme Party

Throw the party of the century! Put a twist on the conventional Halloween party by inviting your guests to come as partyers from a former era. Most people have something in their closet that'll work in a pinch, and each decade offers its own appeal.

1920s: Flapper dresses, cigarette holders, long strands of pearls, bobbed hair, and stretchy headbands for the gals. Men should slick back their hair and dress in their best suits. Drink: gin and tonic.

Inspiration: F. Scott Fitzgerald's *The Great Gatsby*, Clara Bow.

1940s: Wartime fashions featured dames in uniforms or wasp-waisted, broad-shouldered suits (add classic makeup, red lips, curled hair, and seamed stockings) and men in uniform. Play big-band music. Decor should capture a spirit of old-time Americana, and might include the flag itself or vintage war propaganda posters. Rent *Swing Kids* for the costumes, the music, and the dancing.

teen idols. Serve punch (spiked or not). Think *Happy Days, American Graffiti,* and *Grease.*

1960s–1970s: Flower power! Break out your grooviest bell-bottoms, tie-dyes, fringy vests, peace-sign jewelry, round John Lennon shades, Birkenstocks, or your most psychedelic platform shoes. Wear your hair au naturel and parted in the middle. Invite guests to "celebrate Halloween '60s-style" and flash everyone a peace sign as they arrive. Walls should be adorned with MAKE LOVE, NOT WAR posters. You could also hang tapestries or Woodstock memorabilia.

1950s: Poodle skirts, high ponytails, saddle shoes, neck scarves, and angora sweaters are ideal for gals. For guys: Wear a varsity letter sweater. Roll up your dungarees with a wide cuff and slick your hair into a pompadour. Or play the bad-boy type: James Dean with a white T-shirt and black leather jacket. As host, you should play doo-wop tunes, put old records out on display, and hang photos of your favorite

1980s:

There are several ways to play this decade. You can go for the power-hungry corporate executive look, carrying a briefcase and a *Wall Street Journal.* Men should wear their hair slicked sharkishly back (à la Michael Douglas in *Wall Street*); women should look business-conservative yet sexy (big shoulder pads are a must). The invitation could include an image of a bull (as in "bull market"). Decorative touches include silver bowls filled with sugar and Monopoly money strewn about tables. You can also go the new-wave/punk route in neon colors, big hair, and wild clothes. (Girls can add fluorescent makeup and jelly bracelets—think Cyndi Lauper.) Use bold, loud colors in your decor. If you still have cassette tapes or records from the '80s, this is the time to break them out.

CHAPTER FIVE

HALLOWEEN

The trick is to stay alive.

Everyone is entitled to one good scare.

MOUSTAPHA AKKAD PRESENTS "HALLOWEEN"
DONALD PLEASENCE IN JOHN CARPENTER'S "HALLOWEEN"
WITH JAMIE LEE CURTIS, P. J. SOLES, NANCY LOOMIS • DIRECTED BY JOHN CARPENTER
EXECUTIVE PRODUCER IRWIN YABLANS • DIRECTED BY JOHN CARPENTER • PRO

HALLOWEEN
page 125

ELMER FUDD
page 100

HOLLY GOLIGHTLY
page 102

Movie and TV Characters

Tap into Tinseltown history—whether you take your inspiration from the big or small screen, you're sure to have a larger-than-life Halloween!

GILLIGAN'S ISLAND
page 116

LITTLE ORPHAN ANNIE

Find a cherry red, knee-length dress, white knee socks (to be hiked up), black Mary Janes, and a curly red wig. Draw brownish freckles all over your nose and cheeks with an eyeliner pencil. Tote along a stuffed-animal dog, your beloved mutt Sandy. Or convince the father figure in your life to wear a bald cap (see page 75) and his best black suit—your very own **Daddy Warbucks.**

THREE AMIGOS/AMIGAS

A few crucial costume elements to turn you and two buddies into the **Three Amigos** (or **Amigas**). One: you'll need some sombreros (anyone been South of the Border recently?). Two: black mustaches. Three, four, and five: you'll need red bandannas to tie around your neck, fake pistols, and black vests or ponchos to go with your black pants.

Flavor Savers (a.k.a. Mustaches)

Here are some options, should your costume require a little hair above the lip.

- **Grow one**
- **Buy a stick-on from your local drugstore during the pre-Halloween season**
- **Burn a cork and draw one on (Let it cool first.)**
- **Use a black or brown eyeliner pencil (also good for moles, faux freckles, cat whiskers . . . so versatile!)**

BAMBI

Does the quick encroachment of Halloween have you feeling like a deer in headlights? Go with that—dress all in brown, with a tan oval of faux fur pinned on your chest, and a white tail pinned to your bottom. Glue white felt dots to your back for a faunlike appearance. Add brown felt ears. Blacken your nose. For **Rudolph,** Santa's MVR (most valuable reindeer), add antlers and a red nose (use stick blush or a clown nose).

JAMES BOND

In an impeccable tuxedo, with your slicked-back hair, packing a plastic pistol, everyone is sure to guess who you are. But if they don't? Simply tell them, ''Bond . . . **James Bond.**'' More clues: Carry a martini glass and get a girlfriend to dress up as sexy blond Bond girl **Pussy Galore** and hang on you all night. She should carry a plastic pistol, too, and wear a gold vest with a black velvet jacket and pants.

BETTY BOOP

In a curve-hugging, strapless cocktail dress (ideally, either red with white polka dots or basic black), a short black bob, black pumps, and dramatically fake eyelashes (see page 49), you'll be a dead ringer. For anyone who doesn't quite get it, you'll need to do your best with her trademark wiggle and ''Boop-boop-a-doop!''

CHARLIE BROWN/LINUS

You can step out as **Good Ol' Charlie Brown** with little effort: Just cut a strip of black felt in a zigzag pattern (about 3 inches wide), and sew or superglue it to an oversized yellow T-shirt. Then put on a pair of black shorts, yellow socks, and white sneakers. A bald cap (see page 75) makes the look. Don't forget to tote around your Snoopy stuffed animal and a football or a kite. Charlie Brown's friend **Linus** has a striped shirt (black horizontal stripes on a brightly colored background—red, blue, purple), black shorts or pants, and white sneakers. A Great Pumpkin is optional, but a blue security blanket is an absolute necessity.

The Legend of Jack-o'-Lantern

Ever wonder where the ritual of carving a face out of a pumpkin comes from? Maybe you haven't. Truthfully, we never gave it much thought until we stumbled upon this funny Irish myth.

It seems the carving practice originated from a legend about a man nicknamed "Stingy Jack." Living up to his name, Stingy Jack convinced the Devil to cover the tab for his pint of ale by transforming himself into a coin. Once the Devil had done it, however, Stingy Jack decided it'd be better to keep the change. So he tucked the coin inside his pants pocket next to a silver cross, imprisoning the Devil and preventing him from reverting to his natural form. Eventually, Stingy Jack agreed to free Satan, on the understanding that he wouldn't bother Jack for a year and wouldn't claim his soul after death. After that year passed, Jack once again tricked the Devil—by trapping him up in a tree and carving a cross in the trunk to prevent him from climbing down. This time around, Jack negotiated for ten Devil-free years.

When Jack died, God barred such a shady character from entering Heaven. But the Devil held to his promise not to take Jack's soul into Hell, and Jack was sent off into the deep, dark night with one burning coal to light his way. Putting his eternal flame into a carved-out turnip, legend has it that Jack has roamed the earth with his lantern ever since. "Jack of the Lantern," as the Irish dubbed him, gradually became "Jack-o'-Lantern." In England, large beets are often used to hold the candle flame. In America, the native pumpkin became the perfect and popular receptacle.

How to Toast Pumpkin Seeds

After hours of carving and candy intake, some salty, toasted pumpkin seeds may be just what you're looking for. Preheat your oven to 350 degrees. Rinse your seeds free of any pumpkin goop (they don't have to be totally innard-free), and pat them dry. Toss them in a bowl with salt and a bit of olive oil. Spread all the seeds out in a single layer on a cookie sheet, and put them in the oven for 20 to 30 minutes (when they start to look golden, they're done). No need to flip them over—just slide them into a bowl and allow them to cool.

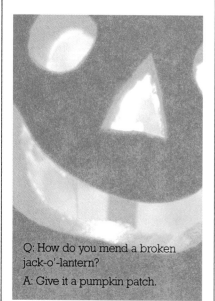

Q: How do you mend a broken jack-o'-lantern?
A: Give it a pumpkin patch.

CHARLIE CHAPLIN

Are you a man of few words? Keep quiet about the costume you're planning to star in this year, or someone might steal your silent-screen idea. Put on a black bowler hat and a black three-piece suit over a white oxford shirt. Blacken your eyebrows, put on some eyeliner, and add an inch-wide mustache (see page 88). Don't forget your cane, and be sure to practice the walk. (Rent *The Kid* and/or *The Circus* if you need a refresher course.)

Pumpkin Carving 101

What would Halloween be without jack-o'-lanterns? It's hard to imagine. Their ghostly glow has illuminated front porches for generations of candy-seeking trick-or-treaters. Here are some tips for creating your own leering lantern.

TOOLS OF THE TRADE

The Basics:

- **a long, thin-bladed knife or a mini saw with serrated edges**
- **a large metal ladle or ice-cream scoop**
- **a short, thin-bladed knife**

Above and Beyond:

- **wood-carving tools**
- **a melon baller**
- **an electric drill**
- **a thin nail or a thick pin**
- **cookie cutters**

PICK OF THE PATCH

Pick your pumpkin carefully! Size and shape *do* matter in the great world of grinning gourds. A medium-sized pumpkin with smooth and round sides is the easiest to carve. It will also produce a tidier, more traditional-looking jack-o'-lantern. However, an irregularly shaped pumpkin with bizarre wartlike growths may produce the horrifying effect you're striving for. Go for it! Just remember, the unique shape of your pumpkin may increase the difficulty of your project. If you find a particularly beautiful or unique pumpkin, you may choose to leave it as is. Uncarved pumpkins make beautiful Halloween centerpieces or around-the-house decor.

GETTING STARTED: THE LOBOTOMY

Okay, sorry for the gross analogy. But the pumpkin *is* the jack-o'-lantern's head, and this is the operation that will leave it with a big permanent grin.

With a long, thin-bladed knife or mini saw, cut a hexagon or pentagon around the stem of the pumpkin (but go with straight lines—circles are practically impossible to cut). Remember that the size of the opening needs to be large enough to stick your hand (and possibly your arm) into, with enough room to move around. As you cut, keep your knife angled a little toward the stem. This will give your lid a cone shape and keep it from falling into the pumpkin. Next, scrape or cut away the meat from the lid until it's only about an inch thick. Then cut a narrow V-shaped notch out of the lid as a "chimney" for the candle's heat and smoke. (You can skip this step if you don't plan to use any kind of flame.)

Using your ladle or ice-cream scoop, spoon out the pumpkin's pulp, strings, and seeds. This can get pretty messy, so be prepared to roll up your sleeves and have some fun. After you have extracted most of the pulp, really work at scraping the meat off the sides of the pumpkin. Like the lid, you want the walls of your pumpkin to be about one inch thick. Don't rush through this stage in anticipation of getting to the carving. Scraping away the meat helps to prolong the life of your pumpkin. Firmer flesh will take a longer time to decompose, and will attract fewer bugs and result in less mildew.

After your pumpkin is hollowed, let the carving begin! First, the design. There are a few ways to go about getting your design onto the pumpkin, and the method you choose will depend on the complexity of your jack-o'-lantern's design and your own level of ability. Here are a few different approaches:

■ First-time or insecure carvers: Go the safe route. Use a stencil and trace your design onto the pumpkin. You can either buy a stencil or create your own out of heavy construction paper. To transfer the stencil's design onto the pumpkin's surface, simply trace its outline with a marker.

■ Ambitious and confident freehanders: If you have a strong vision of your pumpkin's visage, and you're certain you can turn your mental image into reality—why wait? Use a marker to sketch your plan directly onto the pumpkin, and move on to the next step.

■ Practically professional: To transfer extremely detailed designs onto your pumpkin, try this slow but effective method. Draw your design onto a piece of paper, then tape the paper securely onto the pumpkin. Using a thin nail or a thick pin, prick holes into the pumpkin's surface along the design's lines. Then peel away the paper and use your knife to connect the dots.

Once your design is transferred onto the pumpkin's surface, use the shorter thin-bladed knife to cut it out. Make sure you cut from the center of the pumpkin out to the sides. (Cut out the nose first, then the eyes and mouth.) Each time you cut into your pumpkin, its structure gets weaker. By starting from the inside and working out, you are less likely to have a tragic "cave-in." For similar reasons, push the pieces you've cut out from inside the pumpkin. If a piece happens to break off (teeth are especially at risk), don't worry. Reattach the piece by sticking one half of a toothpick into the broken piece, and the other half where it belongs in the pumpkin. After you finish cutting your design, reach inside the pumpkin and scrape away the meat (at about a 45-degree angle) from the edges of your cuts. This will make your lines appear clean and straight.

BEYOND THE BASICS

Melon ballers and carving tools can be used to etch away the skin of the pumpkin, creating an interesting layered effect. Without actually

I am pumpkin—hear me roar!

breaking through to the pumpkin's meat, the etched-away areas will give off an orangy glow. Use an electric drill to create perfectly round holes. Press sturdy cookie cutters into the pumpkin's skin and then cut the shapes out with a knife.

LET THERE BE LIGHT!

For a traditional jack-o'-lantern, go for the flame. A small votive candle placed in a clear glass container will work wonders to illuminate your masterpiece. White candles project more light than other colors. But never leave a burning candle unattended. You want your jack-o'-lantern to attract admirers and trick-or-treaters, not the fire department.

If you decide to use a flashlight, lightbulb, or Christmas lights, remember that these items also get hot and need occasional checkups. The lights shouldn't touch the sides of the pumpkin, so place them on a coffee can or other nonflammable object. Glow Sticks are probably the only completely risk-free lighting method, but you sacrifice brightness (and ambience) when using them.

PUMPKIN PRESERVES

It's a shame to watch your pumpkin wither after you've spent so much time turning it into a work of art. Here are some ideas for keeping your pumpkin around as long as possible.

The number-one reason pumpkins begin to wither and collapse is loss of moisture. After you finish carving your pumpkin, coat the exposed meat with petroleum jelly. Although this turns a messy job into a slippery one, the jelly helps to seal in the pumpkin's moisture and deter wrinkling. Alternatively, you can dunk your pumpkin into a bucket of water overnight to restore some of the moisture lost during the day. Adding a little bleach to the water

will help kill the bacteria and bugs that have started to decompose your master-piece. A dry method of slowing decomposition is to store the pumpkin in your refrigerator at night. But who has room for that in a fridge full of Dirt and Worms Pie (see page 212)? If you are really serious about prolonging your pumpkin's life, there are pumpkin preservation products available at stores and online. Products like Pumpkin Dunk'N claim to give your pumpkin up to two extra weeks of life. For more product information, inquire at your local pumpkin stand, or visit **www.yankeehalloween.com.**

A HAIR-RAISING PUMPKIN

To perfect that frozen-with-fear facial expression, leave your pumpkin's lid off and stick long dried grasses (available at floral

shops or in your backyard) into the head. It will look like the pumpkin's hair is standing on end. Obviously, candles are *not* a smart idea for this pumpkin.

THE PUKING PUMPKIN

Carve a simple jack-o'-lantern face with the mouth hanging open and frowning. When you're finished, arrange the pumpkin's pulp and seeds so that they appear to be pouring out of its mouth. That's what happens when Jack eats too much candy corn and drinks too much wine.

CHEECH AND CHONG

Here's an idea for two-of-a-kind buds: Go as **Cheech and Chong.** Cheech decks out in a low-brim black hat, wife-beater, Hawaiian shirt, baggy pants, and a thick mustache; and Chong also wears a Hawaiian shirt, with a bandanna around his forehead, a beard, some round, wire-rimmed glasses, and blue jeans. Converse Hi-Top sneakers for both.

Hold Your Hair High

Some costumes demand gravity-defying hair. Whether you're stepping out the door as Edward Scissorhands or as the Windy City (see page 179), there are times when you simply *must* be master of your hair. If normal hairstyling products are letting you down, it's time to bring out the big guns. Try egg whites. Use them as you would hair gel. A blow-dryer will set your 'do.

EDWARD SCISSORHANDS

Dressing as **Edward Scissorhands** requires a little makeup artistry. Paint your face and all exposed skin a pasty white with criss-crossing scars (see page 28). Dye your hair with washable jet-black hair dye and use whatever methods (teasing) and products you must to get that fork-stuck-in-an-electrical-outlet look (see opposite). The outfit is a white oxford shirt with black pants and suspenders. For your hands, tie together two bundles of three dull pairs of scissors and then tape one to each wrist (you'll need some assistance). Be careful with the handshakes. (The safer and lighter alternative: Sculpt blades out of cardboard covered with aluminum wrap.)

Better a hair stylist than a dentist.

ELMER FUDD

"**B**e vehwy, vehwy qwiet . . . we're hunting wabbits!" Tiptoe around as goofy, easily fooled **Elmer Fudd** in a red and black flannel coat, brown pants, and hiking boots. You'll also need a bald cap, a hat with earflaps, a plastic hunting rifle, and a rabbit hunting permit (drawn on an index card) pinned to a shirt pocket.

FRED FLINTSTONE

"**Y**abbadabba-doo!" Step out as the prehistoric family man and upright citizen of Bedrock. Pick up some leopard-print fabric at a local sewing shop and make a very rudimentary toga (see page 11), tying at one shoulder. Sew both sides together so you have a knee-length, one-shouldered shift dress. (Yes, **Fred** wears a dress.) Then cut a ragged or zigzag pattern along the bottom edge. Fred should have Birkenstocks, a five-o'clock shadow, and a bowling-ball bag. For wife **Wilma:** red hair done up in a bun, a one-shouldered white dress with ragged hem, and a gigantic beaded choker.

HANS AND FRANZ

"**I** am **Hans.**" "And I am **Franz.**" "And we are here to pump . . . you up!" The steroid-taking German weight lifters, immortalized on *Saturday Night Live* by Kevin Nealon and Dana Carvey, had overstuffed egos, overstuffed torsos, and puny legs. Cut a pair of tight panty hose, and put them on like sleeves to cover your arms from your wrists to your shoulders. Stuff them with anything you've got lying around: pairs of tube socks, toilet paper, you name it. Use wristbands to cover the ends of the panty hose at your wrists. Dress in matching gray sweat suits, with matching pairs of fingerless weight-lifting gloves. Carry a light dumbbell, throw a towel around your neck, and coif your hair into little spikes.

INSPECTOR GADGET

He may be muddleheaded, but he's got fun toys. To get his look, find a belted trench coat, fedora hat, bow tie, and a big magnifying glass. Add gadgets: the extending arm (glue a stuffed rubber glove to a stick, and keep it up your sleeve); the walkie-talkie watch (to speak to your niece, Penny); the umbrella with propellers attached. Creativity is key. Don't forget his key phrase, "Go go gadget."

HOLLY GOLIGHTLY

Audrey Hepburn's elegant *Breakfast at Tiffany's* style may seem inimitable, but you can try your best with a pair of black cigarette pants, black ballet flats, a black sleeveless shirt, a long cigarette holder, and diamond jewelry. Put your brown hair up in a French twist. Powder your face to make it pale, and wear bright red lipstick, and heavy black eyeliner on your upper lids only.

INDIANA JONES

Brown fedora, bullwhip, leather bomber jacket over a white or tan button-down shirt, and khakis.

JUDY JETSON

See your future as a space-age babe? All you need is a short silver miniskirt, a brightly colored top, go-go boots, and white hair pulled into a high side ponytail. Cover your wristwatch in foil and tape a small photo of a cartoon hunk to it—it's a video-phone/ wristwatch.

KARATE KID

Wax on, wax off. Find white pants and a matching white karate robe, and cinch it with a black sash. Add a white headband, with half of a red setting sun on it, around your forehead. Walk around barefoot if you can.

KERMIT THE FROG AND MISS PIGGY

It's not easy being green—not to mention having an enamored Piggy on your back. But dressing as Jim Henson's adorable couple shouldn't be too hard. Start with body and face paint (green and pink, respectively). **Kermit** should then add the following: a green hoodie sweatshirt with huge googly eyes sewn on top and a trench coat. For **Miss Piggy:** a blond, curly wig and fake pig ears and snout are in order. She'll also need a low-cut purple dress, a choker of chunky pearls, a pink boa, long satin gloves, and a little curlicue tail attached to her seat. Miss Piggy should also be prepared to give her beloved Kermie a karate chop if he doesn't return her affection during the night (beats getting a pork chop from her direction, the two old guys in the balcony might say).

CAPTAIN KIRK

Calling all Trekkies! Find a mustard-yellow T-shirt, black pants, and black boots. Use fabric paint to blacken the T-shirt's collar, and pin an *Enterprise* logo of gold fabric edged in black over your heart. Use makeup that's just a little too orange for your skin. Whip out your "communicator" (a flip-top cell phone will do) and touch base with your **Mr. Spock** (dark, matted-down hair, pointy ears, pale skin, blue shirt, black pants, and black boots). Or go as an intergalactic **Star Trek Babe:** tight-fitting leotard top with the *Enterprise* logo, miniskirt, and go-go boots.

KRAMER

To pull off Jerry Seinfeld's zany neighbor, you need a checked blazer, a nonmatching print shirt, brown pants, and brown shoes. Make your wavy hair stand on end, and try to mimic his frenetic mannerisms. Puff on cigars and drink only Cosmos. Get another friend to do the same, wear boxing gloves, and you're **Kramer v. Kramer.**

LADY AND THE TRAMP

Here's a good and simple one for two gal pals. Draw straws: One of you gets to dress up as a refined society dame with pearls, white gloves, tasteful hemline, and a lovely handbag. (Think Grace Kelly.) The other? Fishnet stockings (preferably torn), micro-mini skirt, shirt falling off the shoulder, high heels or go-go boots, teased hair, and plenty of makeup—think Julia Roberts's character in *Pretty Woman*, pre–Richard Gere makeover.

LAVERNE AND SHIRLEY

Here's another fun idea for two best friends (girls, or guys in drag). Laverne will need a monogrammed "L" sweater. They'll both need A-line skirts, big bouffants, and a Shotz beer in hand.

PRINCESS LEIA

Replicate the look that made Luke Skywalker—and countless American men in the *Stars Wars* audience—go weak in the knees. In vogue on Alderaan and the *Millennium Falcon:* a long white flowing robe, cinched at the waist with gold cord, white boots. Most important: the signature fat hair buns on either side of your head. To get the look yourself, divide hair down the middle in back, and tie into two low pigtails. Hair extensions for extra bun heft (your local beauty salon or Halloween store should have something that works) are optional. Make both pigtails into soft, full braids. Wrap the

braid around the base of each pigtail, and fasten with bobby pins. For an extra *Star Wars*-y effect, add a light saber. Here's how: Take an empty roll of wrapping paper and wrap it in iridescent blue cellophane. Add an aluminum foil handle at the base. We know it's *Star Wars* heresy—light sabers are for Jedi Knights only—but tell any *Star Wars* geeks that you're taking girl power to a whole new intergalactic level. May the force be with you!

THE LONE RANGER

Are you a bit of a loner? Dress in all khaki or all pale blue, with a black belt, a white cowboy hat, a thin black mask over your eyes, and of course, two silver pistols in a holster. Hi-ho Silver! (For extra effect, carry a white hobbyhorse as Silver.) A friend with long dark hair can be your sidekick, **Tonto,** the Native American who saved your life. He should dress in light-colored suede (or a good approximation), brown moccasins, and a thick leather band around his forehead.

MAGNUM, P.I.

Check in as the ultimate '80s sex symbol. You'll need jeans, a Hawaiian shirt, white tennis shoes, visible chest hair, a Detroit Tigers cap, and '80s aviator shades. It helps to have curly brown hair, and a thick brown mustache (see page 88) is requisite. This is a perfect excuse to splurge on the fire-engine red Ferrari you've always wanted—it'd be a super prop.

MARILYN MONROE

Who doesn't adore this Hollywood siren? Find a wavy, platinum-blond wig, big white clip-on earrings, some red lipstick, a white halter dress, and white high heels. Along the bottom hem of the dress, sew in a thin piece of wire (see right column for how-to). Then mold the bottom of the hem to capture that famous Marilyn-over-the-subway-grate moment, when the air from the train going by blew her skirt up and showed off her gorgeous gams.

Get Blown Away

You can give an article of clothing the windblown look with the help of a length of wire. In many cases, a wire coat hanger (untwisted with pliers) will work, but check out the wire selection at your local hardware store for greater variety. The heaviness and size of the article of clothing should dictate the thickness of the wire you select. Examine the piece of clothing. If it's a skirt, see if you can slip the wire into a part of the hem and feed it through. You might have to cut a little slit on the inside hem of the skirt. If it's a tie, feed the wire through the edges of the underside. Use clear packing tape to keep the tip of the tie on top of the wire. Scarves are a little trickier. Be prepared to ruin whatever scarf you use. If it's a knit scarf, weave the wire through the fabric along the edges. If it's a woven scarf, muster up your sewing talent and create a hem along the edges wide enough to slide the wire through. Mold to the desired shape.

MARY POPPINS

Here's a *supercalifragilisticexpialidocious* idea for a costume: everyone's favorite British nanny! You'll need a long black umbrella, a long, buttoned-up black overcoat with a fluffy red-and-pink-striped scarf, hair pulled up into a bun under a frumpy black hat, a red carpet bag, sensible black boots, and a bottle of Robitussin (with a spoon) tucked into a pocket.

NORM

Want to go where everybody knows your name? Get recognized as television's favorite beer-guzzling bar fixture, Norm from *Cheers.* You'll probably need to stuff a pillow down your dress shirt to get his portly girth. Put on an ill-fitting sportcoat, a striped tie, and carry your own mug of beer and optional stool.

NORMAN BATES

Dress conservatively in dark slacks, a button-down shirt, and a blazer (no tie). Carry a shower curtain stained with fake blood (red paint) and an oversize plastic knife. Scare other guests by "attacking" them through the curtain.

OSCAR THE GROUCH

C*arefully* cut the bottom off a plastic trash can with a heavy-duty X-Acto knife. Punch four holes along the top rim of the trash can (to suspend it over your shoulders). Paint the trash can silver. Once the paint is dry, step inside the trash can, securing it over your shoulders with clothesline, like overalls. Wear green clothing, green face paint, a bushy brown unibrow, and a surly expression. Be grumpier than you've ever been.

POPEYE

Here's a shortcut to going to the gym: Simply cover your arms in nylon stockings (see Hans and Franz, page 101), and then strategically stuff them to give yourself bulging forearms. Add a white sailor's cap and a short-sleeve navy blue polo shirt, blue pants, a corncob pipe (any light-colored pipe will do), and carry a can of spinach (make a new label for another can if you have to). Draw an anchor tattoo on your forearm with marker, and don't forget to squint one eye. If **Olive Oyl** wants to come along, she's got black hair pulled back into a low bun, button earrings, red lipstick, and a long-sleeved, red, scoop-neck shirt with white lace trim at the sleeves and neck. Her black skirt comes down to the midcalf or ankle, and she's got combat boots on her feet.

ROBERT PALMER GIRL

Take a cue from our leggy friend Mariah, who was born to be a **Robert Palmer girl** (minus the drab attitude). Wear a black minidress and black stilettos, and slick your hair back into a low bun (if your hair's not dark, invest in some temporary hair dye). Your eyes are smoky and smouldering; your lipstick is red and shiny; and your blush is dark, almost brown. Recruit a bunch of friends to do the same. Carry inflatable or real electric guitars.

SMURFETTE

Not sold on a costume yet? Maybe it *is* something to get blue about. Put on a blond wig, a white dress, a white beret or cap, and white pumps. Paint your entire face and all visible skin blue, and replace every adjective in your vocabulary with *smurfy.* You're sure to have a *smurftacular* time!

TARZAN

For a happening swinger: Give yourself a golden glow with self-tanning lotion, sport a loincloth (preferably leopard print), slip on a pair of leather sandals, let your hair go wild, and beat your chest as you tell other bemused guests, "Me, **Tarzan!**" And if there's a significant other in your jungle of love, ask her to go as the more civilized **Jane,** in safari gear and a French twist.

WILLY WONKA

What's more appropriate on a chocolate-laden holiday than going as the candy man himself? Find yourself a purple jacket, lime green pants, a red bow tie, a purple top hat, a cane, and an enormous lollipop (Improvise: His outfit really just needs to be colorful.) Pass out golden tickets to other guests, offering free entrance to your fantastic chocolate factory. Get a shorter friend to dress as a hardworking **Oompa Loompa** (one of your factory workers). He should paint his face and body orange, dye his hair green, and put white greasepaint on his eyebrows; the outfit (again, there's room for interpretation) is a red-and-white-striped shirt, white overalls, white gloves, and brown shoes.

ZORRO

Create a little mystery. The masked crusader wears a black vest, pants, cape, shirt, sash, a black gaucho hat, a thin black mustache and, obviously, a black mask over his eyes. Don't leave home without your dueling sword, and be sure to slash the air with your trademark *Z* whenever you make an exit (just don't hurt anyone).

TV CASTS TO REPLICATE

CHARLIE'S ANGELS

(for a group of three)

Your first decision: original or remake? We vote original. All three girls are '70s chic. Get a fair-haired sex kitten to play **Jill Munroe,** the Farrah Fawcett role, and don't forget the heavily feathered hair. Kate Jackson played **Sabrina Duncan,** the serious, sensible, brainy brunette. Sophisticated brunette **Kelly Garrett,** played by Jaclyn Smith, adds more sex appeal and some comic relief. If you can find matching disco-fabulous pantsuits (with bell-bottoms, natch), you get a gold star. Scarves were also very popular, either around the head like a very tight kerchief, or around the neck. All three of you should carry brightly colored plastic guns, and practice striking your group pose (backs together, guns pointed out) before the night begins.

SEX AND THE CITY

(for a group of four)

Miranda: Short red hair, pale skin, red lips, and a business suit. Carry a baby doll and a briefcase.

Charlotte: Think Junior League. Prim and pretty sweater set, skirt, and kitten heels. Pearls. Curl your long dark hair so it falls in gentle waves. Classic makeup.

Carrie: The most room for fun, because you can throw together virtually anything in your closet (as long as it doesn't match) with a pair of teetering stilettos, and you'll be all set. Just make sure your hair is big and slightly frizzy. Other classic Carrie looks: the nameplate necklace, the Fendi bag, the boy's gym shorts circa 1973, and the perpetual gum chewing (or smoking).

Samantha: For the blond femme fatale who knows she's fabulous and doesn't mind flaunting it. You need a dress with a plunging neckline. Accessorize with the best you've got. Or just bare it all (or almost all) in a lacy teddy. Got a younger hunk you can bring along? If not, don't worry: Your costume will have 'em flocking to you in droves by the end of the night.

THE SOPRANOS

(for a group of eight)

Here's a costume that's sure to intimidate. Get your favorite wise guys together: **Tony Soprano** (black leather jacket, open-necked black or patterned shirt, gold necklace, balding hair brushed back, padding on the stomach); **Christopher Moltisanti** (same, but with more hair and no padding); **"Junior" Soprano** (bald cap, oversized dark-rimmed glasses); **Paulie Walnuts** (hair swept back and white at the temples); and **Silvio Dante** (thick brown hair swept back from the fore-head, jacket and shirt with big lapels, a cross necklace). Everyone except Junior should pack heat, or a brightly colored squirt gun. Convince **Adriana La Cerva** (a lot of jewelry, short sexy outfit, heavy eye makeup, and a glass of white wine) and **Carmela Soprano** (full set of acrylic nails, blonde hair

with big bangs, patterned tight pantsuit, bold jewelry) to come along, and bring **Dr. Jennifer Melfi** (glasses and a conservative skirt suit) for emotional support.

GILLIGAN'S ISLAND

(for a group of seven)

Gilligan: Red rugby shirt with a white collar, light-blue bell-bottom jeans, and white tennis shoes. Short brown hair under a floppy white sun hat. Carry a defective white transistor radio.

Skipper: Blue short-sleeved polo shirt (which might need to be stuffed to achieve the right girth), khakis, blue

tennis shoes, and a black captain's hat.

Thurston Howell III: The millionaire wears a dinner jacket, an ascot, salt-and-pepper hair, and a panama hat. A money clip full of greenbacks (or Monopoly money) is a good added touch.

Lovey Howell: Decked out in a gown, pearls, white gloves, curly white or blond hair, perfect makeup, and a parasol. Carry a martini around.

The Professor: Dressed simply in a white oxford shirt, khakis, and a black belt, the

hunky professor might carry test tubes or have his nose buried in a book.

Ginger: As the resident movie star on the island, redheaded Ginger has an obligation to look Marilyn Monroe–glamorous in gown and full makeup, including false eyelashes. Don't forget the soft, breathy voice.

Mary Ann: Dress as the girl next door in pigtails tied with bows, a bright gingham shirt, and blue-jean short shorts.

I LOVE LUCY

(for a group of four)

Lucy: A wasp-waisted housedress with a full, flared skirt. Feather duster. Red hair, red lips, and fake eyelashes.

Ricky Ricardo: White dinner jacket and black pants.

Baton for directing the band. Microphone. Hair slicked back in a dark pompadour.

Ethel Mertz: Similar dress to Lucy's, but with a hairdo of blondish curls. Pearls.

Fred Mertz: Bald cap. Cardigan sweater and button-down shirt.

THE BRADY BUNCH

(for a group of nine)

Carol Brady: Short, blond, flip hair. Wide collar, polyester pants or miniskirt, a scarf tied around your neck.

Mike Brady: Leisure suit. Carry a T-square (he was an architect, remember?). Find a wig that resembles a tight brown perm.

Boys (Greg, Peter, and Bobby): Bell-bottoms and tight shirts. Heads of thick brown hair.

Girls (Marcia, Jan, and Cindy): The older two have long, straight blond hair, and wear miniskirts with wide-lapelled tops. Cindy has blond, ringlet pigtails and a lisp.

Alice: A robin's-egg-blue housedress plus apron, sensible shoes, and an oven mitt. Hair should be whipped up into a brown beehive.

MOVIE CASTS TO REPLICATE

GREASE!

(for an unlimited number)

For a group that "goes together," go ensemble as the cast of this musical hit. The guys dress up as the 1950s T-Birds—black leather jackets, white T-shirts (with a pack of cigarettes rolled into one sleeve), blue dungarees with wide, rolled-up cuffs, greasy pompadours, and combs tucked into back pockets. For the Pink Ladies, the outfit is tight black pedal pushers, black angora sweaters (or white T-shirts—as long as you all match), with pink scarves and pink satin jackets. Saddle shoes and heavy makeup complete the look. Someone can be "innocent" Sandy in wholesome '50s wear or "trashy" Sandy with big hair, black

Lycra pants, black leather jacket, and black high heels. Someone else can be "sweet" Danny in a letter sweater and slacks.

THE WIZARD OF OZ

(for a group of six)

Dorothy: You'll need two braids tied with blue ribbon, a blue (solid or gingham) dress or a blue apron over a white dress, and a picnic basket with your little dog **Toto** inside. Don't forget your ruby slippers! (Glittery is great, but just about any red shoes will do.)

Cowardly Lion: Wear a shaggy brown sweater and brown pants, and attach a long tan tail to your seat. Fill your hair with gel and mousse until you have a full-blown mane. Attach small brown ears. Paint on whiskers and a black nose (see opposite page for more feline makeup tips). Wear a "badge of courage."

Getting Catty: How to Make Yourself Up as a Feline

With white face paint, trace from the edges of your nose all the way down to your chin, and fill in. Add whiskers and a black tip to the end of your nose with black eyeliner. The rest of your face depends on whether you're a calico, black, or tiger-striped cat. This also works for lions, tigers, and other felines.

Tin Man: Paint your body and face monochromatic silver. Make a cylinder out of poster board, cover it with aluminum foil, and poke four holes in the top so you can attach string and wear it over your shoulders. Find a silver baseball cap or a gray knit hat, or spray paint a large funnel silver. Add red lipstick and a black tip on the end of your nose. Carry a big red construction-paper heart and an unopened (i.e., clean) can of oil.

Scarecrow: Are you the brains of the operation? Dress up in overalls, a flannel shirt, and a straw hat. Stuff straw into pockets and sleeves and under your collar. Draw on big, overdone freckles and add a red tip to your nose. A bandanna around your neck and a diploma in your hand, and you're good to go.

For **Glinda the Good Witch** and the **Wicked Witch of the West,** check out "Witches, Both Wicked and Wonderful," in our Classics section (page 22).

A COMMERCIAL BREAK

There's nothing subliminal about the message of these costumes: fun, creative, unusual Halloween garb.

CALIFORNIA RAISIN

Remember this ad campaign? The raisins wore sunglasses, and the background music was Smokey Robinson's "I Heard It Through the Grapevine." So . . . little Ashley thought it would make a wonderful costume, and her mother agreed. All it took was a black trash bag with a hole cut out for the head, and four holes poked out for arms and legs. Black duct tape closed up any extra holes or rips. Add some tights, any color (since raisins don't actually have legs, there's room for some creative license here), white gloves, some '80s shades, and you're ready to go. A cautionary tale, though, against overstuffing. In the sad but true file: A fellow fifth-grader (we won't name names) mistook Ashley—whose trash bag was plumped up perhaps more than the raisin dress code called for—for a California Grape. Ouch.

THE DENOREX GUY

For the guy who feels most at home in his fluffy bathrobe and slippers—this at-home comparer-of-brands costume is just right for you! Provided, of course, that you also feel comfortable walking around with shaving cream on your head. Put shaving cream (the foam kind, not the gel kind) on both sides of your head, being sure to leave a clear, foam-free, one-inch line down the middle. Now, which side tingles? The Denorex side or the generic Brand-X side? Discuss at length.

DOUBLEMINT TWINS

Double your pleasure, double your fun! If you have a friend who shares your physical features (body type, hair color and length), get matching '70s preppy outfits (khaki shorts, short-sleeved polo shirts). Do your hair the same way (pigtails or ponytails), and carry packs of Doublemint gum. That'll give everyone something to chew on.

GOT MILK?

GOT MILK? A swipe of Desitin—or some other white sticky substance—and you're a **"Got Milk?"** advertisement. Add a "Got Milk?" T-shirt—store-bought or homemade. Show the world you've got strong (if lazy) bones.

HAMBURGER HELPER

HAMBURGER HELPER Dress all in black, with just one white glove on your hand. Draw a red edge on the cuff of the glove. With a black marker, draw a smiley face on your palm.

JOLLY GREEN GIANT AND SPROUT Ideal for a couple who's mismatched in height or a parent-child combo. The gear for both is basically the same. Don green face paint, green tights, a green turtleneck, green gloves, and a short green toga (if you have time, pin green felt leaves to the toga). They also sport leafy green hair: Either temporarily dye your hair green or wrap a fake vine (available at craft stores) around your head and clip it in place. If you don't have green shoes, cover your shoes with pieces of green felt (wrap it around and staple the felt to itself).

"KODAK MOMENTS." Here's a snappy idea for a group of friends. Invest in a dozen disposable cameras, and dress everyone as **"Kodak moments"**— the beaming graduate getting his diploma or posing between his proud parents; the ballerina getting roses tossed at her feet after a stunning stage performance; a kid unwrapping a puppy for Christmas, and so forth. Make up your own—but be sure to capture all these posed moments on film.

MASTERCARD Wear your fanciest skirt (with a sign stuck to it: Chanel, $1000), your fanciest shoes (with a large tag: Manolos, $500), and walk around with toilet paper trailing from your foot marked **"Priceless."**

MR. CLEAN Does the top of your head gleam like a clean kitchen floor? Here's an easy costume for you: You'll need a bald head, a gold hoop earring in your left ear, and white eyebrows (use greasepaint). Wear white shoes if you have them (black if you don't) and a blindingly white T-shirt and pants.

Top 10 Classic Camp Movies

Study the classics for inspiration! In these flicks you'll find suspense, humor, *and* great costume ideas.

The Blob. This cult classic is a must-see for horror flick aficionados. But prepare to suspend disbelief: A gelatinous "blob" from outer space attacks Earth, consuming everything in its path.

Creature from the Black Lagoon. A crew of scientists (and one beautiful fiancée) go on an expedition for an amphibious–human creature in a . . . you guessed it, black lagoon. Bad special effects to match the acting but it's a classic all the same.

Dracula.
This is one of the old "creature features" that prevented Universal Studios from going under in the 1930s, and it's the one that put Bela Lugosi on the map. It's your classic, archetypal vampire movie: A Transylvanian hunts for human blood.

Frankenstein. James Whale's 1931 Hollywood version of the Mary Shelley classic cast a then-unknown Boris Karloff as the staggering, oversized monster.

The Mummy. A team of British archaeologists awaken from the dead an ancient Egyptian mummy, who embarks on a search to find a living bride. Although the 1999 remake has great special effects, Boris Karloff's spooky performance as the mummy Im-Ho-Tep in the original is unmatched.

sharp-fanged Wolf Man to its pantheon of celebrity monsters.

Scary Movie. This parody of formulaic horror movies like *Scream* and *I Know What You Did Last Summer* pokes fun at the genre's predictability, with plenty of juvenile jokes thrown in.

Them! For sci-fi fans, this completely campy 1954 classic about giant, mutated, terrorizing ants (spawned by the effects of atomic testing) is just the ticket.

The Beast from 20,000 Fathoms. An enraged dinosaur, awakened from his slumber by atomic testing, trashes Manhattan in this 1953 sci-fi classic.

Bride of Frankenstein. The sequel to the hugely popular *Frankenstein* is widely considered to be the superior of the two. Boris Karloff stars once more, and his bride—with her tall tower of lightning-streaked hair—gives the film camp appeal (although her on-screen role is brief).

The Wolf Man. This gloomy 1941 version of the classic tells the tale of a young man who goes to visit the estate of his father (played by Claude Rains). Having been bitten by a werewolf, the son undergoes a transformation when the moon is full. The movie was a smash hit, and Universal Pictures added the bushy-haired,

Top 10 Truly Terrifying Movies

Do you like your horror movies to scare you out of your wits? Watching any of the following horror flicks should keep you indoors, covered in blankets, for at least three weeks.

The Shining. On the terror scale, this one rates high. Jack Nicholson plays a struggling writer who signs on to be the caretaker of a summer resort while it's closed for the winter. This Kubrick-directed gem will keep you up at night.

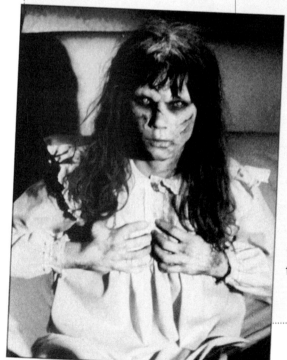

The Exorcist. A young girl (Linda Blair, left) becomes violently possessed, and her desperate mother (Ellen Burstyn) calls in a priest for an exorcism. Taken out of context (the head-twisting, the levitation), the special effects seem dated—but they're still terrifying.

Silence of the Lambs. This harrowing psychological drama will keep you on the edge of your seat. Directed by Jonathan Demme, the film introduces the blood-chilling, psychopathic Hannibal Lecter (Sir Anthony Hopkins, above), who faces off against FBI investigator Clarice Starling (Jodie Foster) in a riveting game of cat and mouse.

Candyman. Not for the faint of heart. This chilling movie is about a student who, while researching urban legends for her thesis, becomes particularly intrigued by the story of the Candyman, the ghost of a black man, brutalized and killed for loving a white woman, who slays anyone who dares to utter his name.

Halloween. This film marked the beginning of the slasher movie era, with the original scream queen played by Jamie Lee Curtis. In this movie and the sequels that follow, psychotic Michael Meyers strikes fear into the heart of suburbia by attacking in the one place where people feel most comfortable and relaxed—at home. The film spawned a sea of imitators.

Nightmare on Elm Street. Wes Craven's bloodcurdler about serial killer Freddy Krueger (below), who terrorizes the dreams of a group of

teenaged friends. Freddy's signature look: a deeply scarred face and blades instead of fingers.

When a Stranger Calls. In this suspenseful nail-biter, a baby-sitter (Carol Kane) gets repeated phone calls from a homicidal maniac, and then finds that the children in her care have been brutally murdered. She narrowly escapes with her own life. Years later, when the heroine is a mother herself, the slayer escapes from a mental institution and tries to kill her children.

Friday the 13th. This marked the introduction of killer psycho Jason Voorhees, also the evil behind eight sequels. All the basic mechanics of the '80s movie are in place here: a group of sexy teenagers in a remote location. Look for a young Kevin Bacon.

Cape Fear. Martin Scorsese's remake of the 1962 thriller (below). Robert De Niro stars as a serial rapist, recently released from prison, who wants revenge on his attorney, played by Nick Nolte, for making a halfhearted attempt to plead his case. He goes after Nolte's wife (Jessica Lange) and daughter (Juliette Lewis).

The Blair Witch Project. A faux documentary about three filmmakers investigating the notorious Blair Witch. Although often parodied for its wobbly, handheld camera technique, some find the movie all the more frightening because it seemed unstaged.

CHAPTER SIX

**JACKIE
KENNEDY ONASSIS**
page 135

MICK JAGGER
page 132

Celeb Sightings

Red carpet—here you come! Get your fifteen minutes as one of these famous figures, and bring along a pen for autographs. Your adoring fans will know you're the real deal when they see you.

JUDGE JUDY
page 132

PAMELA ANDERSON

Want to show a little skin? **Pamela Anderson** couldn't be easier (legal note: as costume, not as person). Got a red bathing suit? Check. Heavily padded strapless bra underneath? Check. Platinum blond wig? Check. Drawn-on chain-link tattoo around the bicep? Check. Wear flip-flops and a whistle around your neck. And if you're itching for a fight, get your guy to dress up as ex-hubby **Tommy Lee** —complete with body art, white wife-beater, bandanna, ripped jeans, and a black leather jacket.

DALAI LAMA

Serenity now! Achieving inner balance and a cosmic understanding ain't so easy. But *dressing* like you've got them is a snap. Step 1: Shave your head, or you can just opt to wear a bald cap (see page 75)—but really, where's your Halloween spirit? Step 2: Dig up a maroon skirt and yellow shirt. Drape a maroon cloth under your right arm and over your left shoulder. Step 3: Wear sandals or flip-flops, a pair of wire-rimmed glasses, and a set of prayer beads around your left wrist.

THE BEATLES

Relive the British Invasion by dressing up as the early **Beatles:** George Harrison (guitar), Ringo Starr (drumsticks), Paul McCartney (bass guitar), and John Lennon (guitar). You'll all need bowl haircuts (or wigs), and dark suits with white shirts and very skinny black ties.

JERRY GARCIA

Make all the Dead Heads in your life happy. Give yourself gray hair and a bushy, gray beard. Don a tie-dyed T-shirt (stuffed with a pillow), jeans, a guitar, and wire-rimmed glasses, and you're the late, great lead singer of The Grateful Dead. For added authenticity, bend the ring finger on your right hand at the knuckle and tape it down.

JANE GOODALL

Put on your jungle gear and commune with our furry cousins. Pull your dirty-blond hair into a ponytail, put on khaki pants and shirt and brown hiking boots, and carry a pair of binoculars, a journal for diligently taking notes, and most important, a stuffed chimpanzee. You're the spitting image of the renowned anthropologist.

JACKSON 5

Going as the **Jackson 5**—Jackie, Tito, Jermaine, Marlon, and Michael—is as easy as ABC. Match Afro wigs with some seriously retro '70s gear (think brown and orange polyester, wide lapels, and platform shoes). Or you and a friend could dress as **Michael then** and **Michael now. Michael then** was adorable in a leisure suit and a microphone. **Michael now** is in a red faux military jacket with a white T-shirt underneath, skintight black pants, and one glove. His hair hangs in slick tendrils around his face, which is palest white. Tasteless prop: Carry a baby doll, and at various times throughout the night, hold it at arm's length (as if over a balcony).

MICK JAGGER & JERRY HALL

A hot costume for a rock 'n' rollin', on-again, off-again couple. **Mick** wears a Stones T-shirt, a blazer with the sleeves rolled up, blue jeans, and mussed-up hair. **Jerry** needs a long blond wig, a white cowboy hat and boots, a slinky, low-cut gown, and bright-red lipstick. Variation for two guys: **Mick Jagger and Keith Richards.** Dress code for both is skintight rocker-fabulous. Keith wears a black leather jacket, shades, small hoop in his left ear, a few beaded necklaces, a bandanna wrapped around his forehead. The ever-present cigarette

adds a touch of authenticity, as does makeup that emphasizes Keith's years of hard living (see page 34). If you've got girlfriends who want in on the action, ask them to dress up as manic **groupies,** complete with autograph book, signed pictures, and tossable undergarments.

JUDGE JUDY

B e a teeny-weeny meanie justice machine. You'll need a black robe, a gavel, pearls, granny glasses, and all the 'tude you can muster.

EVEL KNIEVEL

Halloween's a time to be daring, so who better to dress up as than the world's greatest daredevil? You'll need a crash helmet, aviator shades, black gloves, and a white or red jumpsuit with any combination of the Stars and Stripes down each arm and leg.

MONICA LEWINSKY

A favorite in the late Clinton era. Long-sleeved navy blue cocktail dress, black wig, some shaving cream on the shoulder, and a cigar. The most infamous intern ever.

MADONNA

Get a group of gals to go as different stages of Madge's evolution. There's the **Material Girl,** in a long, pink satin gown, elbow-length gloves, platinum blond hair, a mink stole, and lots of diamonds. Or be the punky rebel from **Papa Don't Preach** (short blond hair with dark roots, black leather jacket, black pants, and boots). The sacrilegious beauty in **Like A Prayer** wears her hair dark and wavy, and sports a black slip with a cross around her neck. There's also the **cone-shaped bra** phase; the **urban cowboy** phase (wavy blond hair, blue or red cowboy hat, satin cowboy shirt, white jeans, and cowboy boots); and the current **yogi/mother/authoress** phase, for which you could carry a yoga mat, a stuffed teddy bear, and a copy of her book.

LIZA MINNELLI

Liza's back! The shy need not apply: The cabaret star's signature look is a sleeveless black bodysuit, little black hot pants, fishnets, black patent-leather heels, bowler hat, pale skin, silver eye shadow, fake black lashes, and red lipstick. Carry a microphone. Kick up your heels, and give everyone "jazz hands." There's no business like show business!

JACKIE KENNEDY ONASSIS

Fashion icon and arbiter of the '60s, **Jackie O's** trademark style is still as chic as it gets. Give your hair some lift by curling, ratting, and then combing it over. Then wrap your head in a brightly colored Hermès (or faux Hermès) scarf and don some oversize black sunglasses. A simple black shift dress, some big pearls, and good shoes, and you've captured that First Lady panache.

DOLLY PARTON

Halloween's but once a year, so be as double-D as you wanna be. What better reason to stuff your bra silly than your **Dolly Parton** costume? Find a tight dress or shirt and jeans to show off your new cleavage, a white cowboy hat, high heels, plenty of makeup and rhinestones, and a white-blond curly wig.

ELVIS PRESLEY

Want to spark rumors of another **Elvis** sighting? To impersonate the King properly, you'll need a white sequined suit, white shoes, a wide-lapel red shirt, gold chains, dark shades, and plenty of hair grease to mold your (black) hair into his trademark pompadour and chops. Munch on a bacon and peanut butter sandwich, if you dare. And then twitch, shake, and gyrate those hips.

AXL ROSE

Live out your rock star fantasies this year by going as the quintessential bad boy of rock 'n' roll (and Guns N' Roses). The look: every inch of exposed skin covered in tattoos, long stringy hair, bandanna tied around your forehead, white wife-beater, unbuttoned flannel shirt, and skintight pants. Twirl your micro-phone around with gusto.

DIANA ROSS

The original Motown diva presents an excellent dress-up opportunity. Find an evening gown that captures the glamor of the sixties (miniskirts, sheath dresses, lots of polyester and chiffon). Don't forget the matching shoes. Make your hair big, don super-glittery jewelry, and enough mascara to rival Tammy Faye Baker. Finally, what diva would be caught without her microphone? Belt out some of her hits a cappella—"You Can't Hurry Love" and "I'm Coming Out" are classics.

JOHNNY ROTTEN

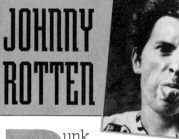

Punk out as the lead singer of the Sex Pistols. If your hair's not naturally red, use a temporary dye to make it so; gel it into spikes. Outfit: a colorful plaid jacket, a ripped-up long-sleeved shirt, tight ripped jeans, and combat boots. Bandmate **Sid Vicious** has dark spiked hair to match his spiked dog collar, ripped jeans, combat boots, a black leather jacket, and no shirt. Carry a bass guitar. Add safety pins wherever you can fit 'em. Don't forget to snarl.

HOWARD STERN

Shock and awe: Dress up as the "king of all media," **Howard Stern.** Wear a long, curly, dark wig, dark circular shades, headphones, black jeans, combat boots, and a black T-shirt underneath an oversize button-down. Ask a pal to go as faithful radio partner **Robin Quivers.** She should wear dreadlocks, headphones, and a forgiving smile.

TINA TURNER

Submitted by our friend Kate: "At age eight, I was **Tina Turner.** I got decked out in a sparkly, sassy Motown-era dress and wore my mom's oversized silver-sequined heels. Teased my hair out about half a foot on each side and sprayed it a darker brown, with gold highlights (for a streaky effect). I put on bright, poppy-red lipstick and I was all set!"

"What's love got to do with it?"

Props Worth Buying

We generally advocate a cheap, do-it-yourself approach to most props, but some Halloween investments are worthwhile.

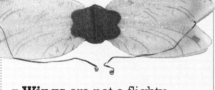

■ **Wings** are not a flighty impulse buy—they come in handy if you're an angel, an insect, or a fairy.

■ Likewise the versatile **crown:** You can be a Queen Bee, a Monarch Butterfly, King Kong, a Royal Pain, or the Queen of Hearts.

■ You'll never regret plunking down a few dollars for a **witch's hat:** At 6 P.M. on October 31, when the first trick-or-treaters ring the doorbell, you can just throw on your hat for an instant touch of the festive spirit.

■ Various **animal ears** are cheap and widely available: cat, puppy, rabbit, and antennae (not really ears, but close enough).

■ **Black hair dye** (temporary) is another good item to have on hand. For the blonds and redheads of the world, no

fair-haired Dracula, Tommy Lee, or Elvira will fly.

■ A brightly colored plastic **squirt gun** will hold up your Shooting Star, your Annie Oakley, and your Tony Soprano.

Top 10 Halloween Tunes

Rock out in the Halloween spirit with these favorites of ours:

- **"Thriller,"** Michael Jackson
- **"Monster Mash,"** Bobby "Boris" Pickett and the Crypt-Kickers
- **"Werewolves of London,"** Warren Zevon
- **"Spooky,"** Santana
- **"Black Magic Woman,"** Santana
- **"Witchcraft,"** Frank Sinatra
- **"I Want Candy,"** The Strangeloves
- **"Abracadabra,"** The Steve Miller Band
- **"Super Freak,"** Rick James
- **"Ghost,"** Indigo Girls

VANILLA ICE

This lip-synching, goofy rapper never goes out of style as a costume, especially if you're blond. Dig out those parachute pants (in a pinch, you could wear acid-wash jeans—c'mon, we know you've still got 'em). Throw on a matching baggy, unzipped sweat-shirt jacket, a gold chain with an enormous dollar sign, the biggest basket-ball sneakers you can find, and spike your hair straight up.

CHAPTER SEVEN

Literature and Arts

ARTIST
page 143

For the Halloween intellectual, might we suggest going as your favorite literary luminary or work of art? Or you could simply take a page from our book.

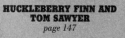

HUCKLEBERRY FINN AND TOM SAWYER
page 147

FRIDA KAHLO
page 149

THE THINKER
page 156

ALICE IN WONDERLAND

Fall through the looking glass as Lewis Carroll's beloved heroine. A blue dress with a white apron, black Mary Janes with white knee socks, and blond hair pulled pack in a black headband. Nibble on "magic mushrooms" and adorable petits fours with "Eat me" tags, and tote around a stuffed animal White Rabbit with a pocket watch.

AMERICAN GOTHIC

Get out yer pitchfork, dear, 'cause we're going as the couple from Grant Wood's famous painting! Remember the rigid portrait of a farmer and his spinster daughter, posed flatly in front of their Iowa farmhouse? He wears overalls, a white collarless button-down shirt, a black blazer, and carries a pitchfork (a rake is a lighter and safer alternative). She's less than fetching in a drab black dress with a cameo pin at the collar, hair pulled back into a low bun. Don't smile.

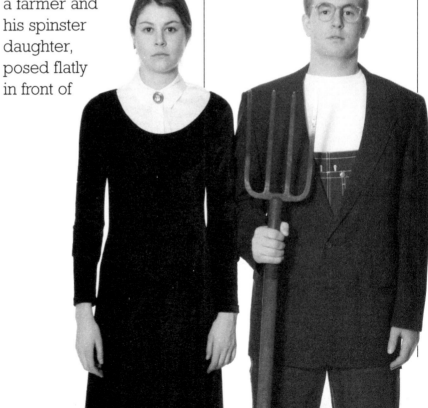

ARTIST

We are all artists within. Let yours come out by slipping on a paint-spattered smock and a beret. Take up your brush, put some paint on your palette, and pour yourself onto the canvas.

BLUE MAN GROUP

For the impulsive drummers: Wear black long-sleeved T-shirts, pants, and shoes, and blue gloves. Put on bald caps (see page 75) and paint any visible skin (including the bald cap) with blue greasepaint. Carry drumsticks and drum on every possible surface. Don't speak a word.

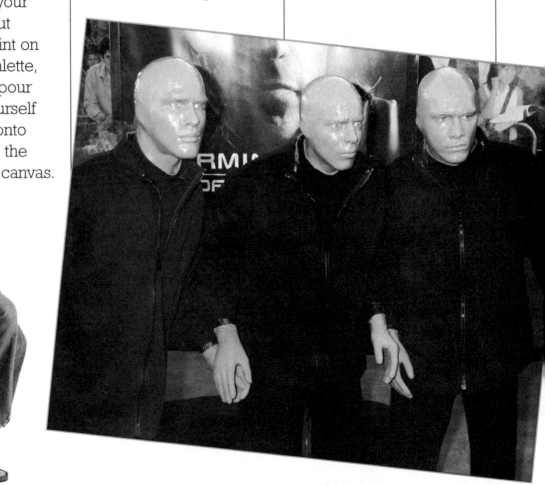

DAISY BUCHANAN

As Jay Gatsby's love interest in F. Scott Fitzgerald's classic *The Great Gatsby*, **Daisy** epitomizes the distinct style of the Roaring '20s. She wears a longish, drop-waisted flapper dress, a feather boa, lace-up high-heeled boots for jitterbugging up a storm, and long pearls, falling to the navel and knotted once at the chest. Her hair is short, slick, and curled around the ear. Her eyelashes are false, but her makeup is otherwise understated. She carries a cigarette holder and a constant fluteful of prohibited champagne.

CAT IN THE HAT

To dress as Dr. Seuss's beloved troublemaker, sport a white turtleneck under black overalls and draw enormous whiskers on your face (see page 119). Add store-bought cat ears and tail. It will be much easier to buy the oversized top hat than to make it, but if you can't find a red-and-white-striped one, you can doctor a black one. Use red and white duct tape to create the stripes. Start with the brim, which should be white, and then move up from there. The first stripe will be red.

DAVY CROCKETT

Born on a mountaintop in Tennessee. . . . If you've got a coonskin cap, and can get your hands on a tan suede fringe jacket and jeans, consider exploring new territory as the king of the wild frontier. Add a canteen and anything resembling a musket to complete the look.

EMILY DICKINSON

Give yourself some poetic license. Wear a floor-length black dress, black choker, and lace-up black boots. Your skin should be pale, and your hair parted down the middle and pulled into a low bun. Carry a black leather journal, and write pensively in it throughout the night. If anyone asks who you are, answer in Emily's own verse:

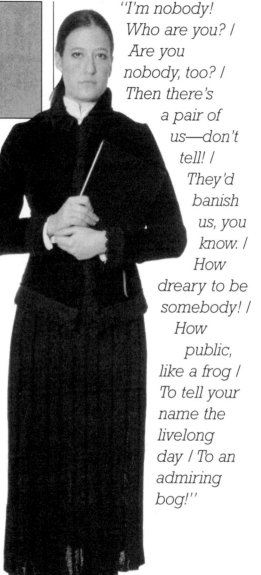

"I'm nobody! Who are you? / Are you nobody, too? / Then there's a pair of us—don't tell! / They'd banish us, you know. / How dreary to be somebody! / How public, like a frog / To tell your name the livelong day / To an admiring bog!"

ALBERT EINSTEIN

Here's a genius idea, if we do say so ourselves. Wear a rumpled tweed suit or a white lab coat, make your hair white and wild, and glue on a big white mustache with spirit gum. Carry around a copy of *The World As I See It*.

ELOISE

Leave the Plaza for a night of Halloween adventure as Kay Thompson's quirky and beloved heroine. You'll need a knee-length black pleated skirt, suspenders, a white blouse with a Peter Pan collar, a pink hair bow, white knee socks and Mary Janes. Looking for a mother-daughter combo? Dress yourself as Eloise's **Nanny** in a plain knee-length skirt (pin a small pillow to your bum to make Nanny's signature bustle), button-down cardigan, lace-up brown shoes, reading glasses, and a low bun.

A book for precocious grown-ups, about a little girl who lives at The Plaza Hotel

KAY THOMPSON'S

ELOISE

DRAWINGS BY HILARY KNIGHT

HUCKLEBERRY FINN AND TOM SAWYER

Mark Twain's irascible hero **Huckleberry Finn** and his pal **Tom Sawyer** are a great duo for two little boys. Suit 'em up in faded overalls, flannel shirts, straw hats, and drawn-on freckles. Lash together a makeshift raft (it doesn't have to be river-worthy) from spare pieces of wood for the boys' epic journey down the Mississippi.

HAMLET AND OPHELIA

Add some drama to your evening. The Prince of Denmark needs a pair of tights, a tunic, a crown, and a fake skull to hold and ponder. The drowned Ophelia should wear pale makeup, have wet-look hair, and fish tank weeds (from a pet store) added to her hair and clothing. A ragged white nightgown will work.

LAURA INGALLS

Don't feel like loading on the glitz and glamor this Halloween? Jump onto this covered wagon and go as the spunky young heroine of *Little House on the Prairie*. Wear plain, homespun clothes: a long skirt, an apron, and brown lace-up boots. Your long hair should be in two braids and capped by a simple bonnet. Carry some schoolbooks and a slate tied together with a simple brown leather belt.

JULIET

"**R**omeo, Romeo, wherefore art thou, Romeo?" Resurrect poor **Juliet** this Halloween. You'll need a long, flowing gown with an empire waist and billowing sleeves; hair parted in the middle and pulled into a low, dramatic bun; a valentine to Romeo in one hand, a vial marked "poison" in the other.

FRIDA KAHLO

Demonstrate your art appreciation by dressing as a Spanish señora—white peasant blouse tucked into a long, layered black skirt; big earrings; brightly colored scarf either tied as a belt or used as a shawl. Pull your hair, parted in the middle, into a bun at the nape of your neck. Use some eyeliner to connect your eyebrows into that signature unibrow (unless you've got one already!), and you're **Frida Kahlo.** If you have one of those stuffed monkeys with velcro paws, carry him around your neck. Hold a paintbrush and palette if you think fellow partygoers will need further clues.

THE LITTLE PRINCE

Dress your boy in a purple, regal-looking cape or a military overcoat, and let him carry around a small telescope. He's Antoine de Saint-Exupéry's diminutive but stout-hearted hero.

MONA LISA

Create a sturdy frame out of cardboard (or buy an inexpensive wooden one), make it large enough for your head and shoulders, and paint it gold. Carry the frame around and pose in the center with long, dark hair, a long, dark dress and shawl, and an enigmatic smile. You're Leonardo da Vinci's masterpiece.

ODYSSEUS

Have some adventures as Homer's hero. Throw on a tunic and some sandals. Carry a toy boat, sword, and shield. Regale your friends with stories of how you single-handedly blinded a Cyclops.

OLD MAN AND THE SEA

For two bookish types: One person dresses as an old man, complete with cane, white hair, and hearing aid. The other wears all blue, with an enormous *C* painted on his chest. Together, you're Ernest Hemingway's famous novel of man's struggle against a force of nature.

PINOCCHIO

We're not lying when we promise that this costume will be a hit. Dress up in shorts and matching suspenders, a white short-sleeved button-down shirt, a little cap, brown shoes, and a prosthetic nose. Attach sturdy wires (untwisted coat hangers) to your shoulders, and stand the wires straight up in the air, as if they're going up and out of sight. A great costume for a real boy.

JACKSON POLLOCK PAINTING

Turn yourself into a masterpiece! Find a white T-shirt and a pair of white pants that you can turn into your canvas. Spread out a lot of newspaper or a drop cloth. (Making this costume is fun, but messy.) Then get out your brushes and paints (they may need a little thinning to make them splatter-perfect—experiment on a piece of newspaper first). Dip your brush, stand back, flick your wrist, and start splattering! Use as many colors as you want—you'll know when you achieve that perfect Pollock look.

HARRY POTTER

There's sure to be a lot of little wizards scurrying about for many Halloweens to come, now that J. K. Rowling has become a household name and her books a universal must-read. You'll need round-rimmed spectacles, black pants and a white oxford shirt, a bow tie, and a pointy wizard's hat. The real trick will be finding Harry's signature crimson and gold scarf. If you don't already have one, you might have to buy it at a costume shop.

HESTER PRYNN

Dress in stern Puritan garb (something resembling a potato sack), lace-up boots, and a shawl or a long, dark cloak. Pull your hair back into a bun and put it under a bonnet. Pin a big, red, felt "A" to your chest. You're the persecuted adulteress from the classic Nathaniel Hawthorne novel, *The Scarlet Letter.*

NURSE RATCHETT

Dressing as a **Nurse** (in all white, including shoes, with a stethoscope and hat) is a classic Halloween choice. But add a bullwhip or a megaphone and some terrifying bedside manners, and you're the drill sergeant in charge of the mental ward in *One Flew Over the Cuckoo's Nest.*

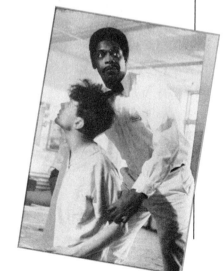

Top 10 Halloween Books

There's nothing better than curling up on a brisk autumn night with a good book. For Halloween spirit, we recommend the following:

1. *It*, Steven King
2. *Collected Stories*, Edgar Allen Poe
3. *The Gashlycrumb Tinies*, Edward Gorey
4. *Frankenstein*, Mary Shelley
5. *The Turn of the Screw*, Henry James
6. *Sweets: A History of Candy*, Tim Richardson
7. *Scary Stories To Tell In The Dark*, Alvin Schwartz
8. *The Witches*, Roald Dahl
9. *Campfire Stories, Vol. 1: Things That Go Bump In The Night*, William Forgey
10. *Interview with the Vampire*, Anne Rice

STARRY NIGHT

Wear all black and wrap yourself with a battery-operated string of white lights. You're not just any old starry night sky, you're van Gogh's ***Starry Night*** painting.

THE THINKER

Deep in thought, trying to come up with just the right costume? How about Rodin's famous sculpture? All it takes is a full-body paint job in gray, including gray spandex shorts . . . and then strike the meditative pose.

CHAPTER EIGHT

The Sporting Life

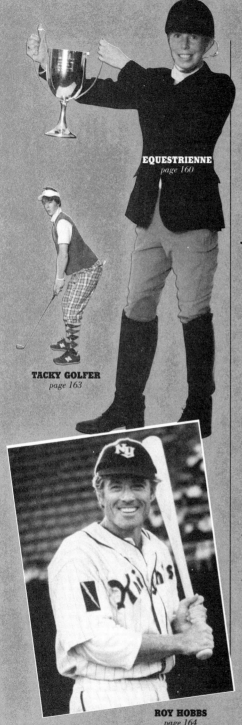

EQUESTRIENNE
page 160

TACKY GOLFER
page 163

ROY HOBBS
page 164

CHEERLEADERS
page 159

If you're an athlete or just a fan, here are several simple costume ideas that go the extra mile. Of course, you can adapt any of these to reflect your favorite sports hero. This is just a starting lineup.

ARCHER AND TARGET

One pal dresses as an **archer** (think either camouflage or Robin Hood) with a child's toy bow and suction cup arrows, and the other wears a **target board.** (Either wear a store-bought target or make one yourself out of cardboard and paint or markers.)

For the finishing touch, attach a suction cup arrow to the target-wearer's forehead with spirit gum. If you want to go the extra mile, lose the target and strap an apple to your head instead. Now you're William Tell.

PRIMA BALLERINA

Doesn't every girl dream of being a **prima ballerina?** Well, Halloween's your chance to make good on those dreams deferred: Find a pink tutu (or a pink leotard with a filmy pink skirt), pink tights, and a pair of pink toe shoes. Pull your hair back into the tightest bun you can stand. Plié and jeté to your heart's content.

BASEBALL DIAMOND

Score a home run! Dress all in green and attach a small (about 2 inches square), white, house-shaped "home plate" (made of white poster board or paper) to your forehead, two square plates to your shoulders and one to just above your belly button. Put a white rectangle on your chin and call it the pitcher's mound. Make a tiny bat and ball from cardboard and pin them on to the "field."

CHEERLEADER

This costume idea makes us say "Rah! Rah!" (That's **Cheerleader** for "Great! Cute costume!") You're probably well acquainted with the basics, but just to jog your memory: pom-poms are ideal, likewise the short, brightly colored pleated skirt, letter sweater or jacket; pigtails, face paint (with your old high school letters, or any other sign of school spirit), ankle socks, and white tennies or saddle shoes. That's right, girls, give us a T-R-I-C-K or T-R-E-A-T!

'80S EXERCISE INSTRUCTOR

Let's get physical. Don a high-cut leotard (the more iridescent the better), brightly colored tights, wristbands, leg warmers, and sneakers. Put your hair into a high ponytail and add a terry cloth headband. . . . Feel the burn!

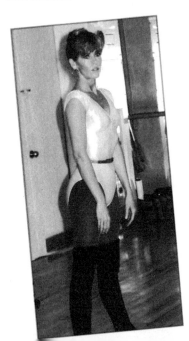

EQUESTRIENNE

Take your cue from **equestrienne** Ashley, and go as a graceful, classic horseback rider this year. The outfit: tight beige pants or jodhpurs, tall black boots, a white turtleneck and a navy-blue blazer. Added touches: a trophy, a riding crop, and a black velvet riding helmet. If you attend a party with a polo player (page 167), you can be **Camilla Parker-Bowles** and **Prince Charles.**

EXTRA POINT

Touchdown! Now earn the **extra point** with this inventive costume for a football fan. Dress in black pants and a black long-sleeved T-shirt or turtleneck. Raise your arms so they're parallel to the floor, then bend your elbows 90 degrees. Ask someone to use white tape to make a line from one of your elbows to the other, from your elbows to your wrists, and down the center of your body from the first tape line to your pelvis. The tape should look like field goalposts. Carry a pigskin, and let others test their kicking talent. (If you're going to encourage this type of crowd participation, we recommend that you wear a mouth guard. Or invest in a Nerf football.)

FENCER

Still on the fence about what to be this year? If you can get your hands on a **fencer's** getup, it makes for a great costume. All white, with a protective mask (easily converted into a **beekeeper** costume next year), and an épée. Touché!

FENWAY FRANK SELLER

Submitted by our friend Shannon: "My best costume was a **Fenway frank seller.** I wore a Red Sox T-shirt, white turtleneck, and blue jeans, with a white canvas Red Sox hat and my hair in a low, side ponytail out the bottom (it was the '80s). I took an empty, shallow cardboard box used for transporting cans of soda (rectangular shape) and attached a big strap to it to put around my neck. I put hot dogs with mustard and relish in the box under plastic, and we secured the plastic to the box so that none of my adventurous classmates could eat the raw hot dogs and get sick. I won second prize at my middle school Halloween party, but sadly, no boys asked me to dance at this affair since the box would have gotten in the way. The class floozy [name withheld] wore a French maid's costume and got a kiss of the same provenance, while I was left with a bunch of raw dogs. No, I'm not scarred or anything."

THE FINISH LINE

And a first place finish for easiest costume goes to . . . you and a friend holding up a piece of ribbon between you as **the finish line!**

TACKY GOLFER

Fore! Who has time to perfect his or her swing? And are those conservative clothes you wear around the course further disincentive, or what? But taken to an extreme, they do make for a funny costume. Pull out your loudest plaid pants, a yellow polo shirt, green sweater-vest, and argyle socks. If you don't have golf shoes, see if you can dig up a pair of Oxfords with a fringe (or make a fringe from paper). Add a blue-tinted visor and a golf bag with a few clubs in it, and hit a hole in one as the **tacky golfer.**

HEISMAN TROPHY

So you were a 98-pound weakling in high school. You sat on the bench for your high-school football team. Coach never called you by the right name. Time to stop wallowing, third string! Halloween affords you a unique opportunity to be a trophy man. Even if you never got your varsity letter, you can embody the pinnacle of accomplishment in amateur football by becoming the

Heisman Trophy! Break out that old football uniform and spray paint it a triumphant gold color. Spray paint a football, too. Smear your body and face with gold body paint, and spray your hair with gold hairspray (available at beauty-supply stores). When anyone asks what you are, strike the signature Heisman pose.

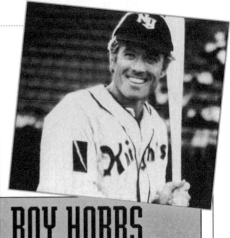

ROY HOBBS

The Natural, the timeless novel by Bernard Malamud, was made into one of our favorite flicks. Robert Redford is the all-American comeback kid who struggles against adversity to make a triumphant return to professional baseball. Write "Wonderboy" and draw a lightning bolt on a wooden baseball bat. Put on a baseball uniform, and sling the bat over your shoulder. Then add some Big League Chew and a pair of cleats, and you'll be a crowd favorite.

ICE SKATER

Double axels and triple lutzes may take years of practice to pull off—but looking like an Olympic **ice skater** is as easy as tying your laces. Start with control-top panty hose. Add a shiny leotard (you can find one in the athletic wear department of any department store) and add a tiny flouncy skirt—one that falls *just* low enough. Wear either your skates with the blade guards on or sneakers, and toss your skates over one shoulder. Pull your hair into a tight, slick bun, and cover your face in vivid makeup. Last touch: Cover the lid of a can of tennis balls with aluminum foil (okay, we're only going for the silver here). Glue your "medal" to a thick blue ribbon, and wear it proudly around your neck. And speaking of figure skating, why not go as one of the sport's more memorable duos? Give **Tanya Harding** big bangs and a hammer, and **Nancy Kerrigan** a bandaged knee and crutches.

CBS
LILLEHAMMER 94

IRON MAN

Not to be confused with Dorothy's cohort, the Tin Man, the **Iron Man** is a tribute to a triathlon that requires *über* athletes to run a full marathon, swim 2.4 miles, and bike 112 miles. To pull all these looks together, wear a singlet with a race number pinned on the front or back, sweatband and running shoes, a swimsuit and goggles, and a bike helmet and fingerless cycling gloves. Having trouble pulling everything together? You can bet it's much harder to pull off the real thing.

ANNA KOURNIKOVA

T his blond, blue-eyed tennis star may be an import (and may not win many matches), but she's as all-American sexy as they come. Why not serve it up yourself? All it takes is a long blond wig (perhaps in a braid), tennis whites (preferably with an Adidas logo and a bit of midriff showing), sneakers, pearl earrings and necklace, a racket, and you've got game.

POLO PLAYER

T his is similar to our Equestrienne costume (see page 160). Wear beige jodhpurs or pants, tall black boots, a polo shirt, and a black riding helmet. Carry a polo mallet and wait for the paparazzi to snap away. Don't let them know you're not really British royalty.

RICHARD SIMMONS AND HIS SWEATIN' TO THE OLDIES GANG

This costume can be hilarious—especially for those involved—if done right. One person needs to volunteer for Richard duty . . . c'mon, how often does the opportunity to wear teeny-tiny short shorts, a tank top, and a curly brown wig present itself?

Not often (we hope). Following Richard's lead, the rest of the group sports as much terry cloth as they can find. We're talking wristbands, leg warmers, headbands, shorts, tank tops. Pin towels around your tummy and hips to add a little girth, then drape some white gym towels around the shoulders. Wear white Reeboks.

One gang member keeps a boom box on her shoulder for the evening and djs the group's dance-a-thon selection (for authenticity, make '50s doo-wop the staple). At the sight of your thrashing, well-padded pack of friends, we guarantee that others will break out into a cold sweat.

SUPER FAN

This is one for the *Monday Night Football*-loving guy. Go out and buy some face paint in your favorite team's colors. We think you probably know the drill from here, but in case you need some guidance, we recommend: stripes down your face, an oversize jersey, a big foam "We're No. 1" finger, a team hat or beer helmet, a hot dog in a bun, and a poster board with a special message to your favorite player. You are a **super fan!**

TENNIS PRO

Serve up some fun in your tennis whites and sweatband. Use your tennis racquet judiciously throughout the evening to share snacks with friends on the opposite end of the couch.

YOGI

Find serenity now as a deep-breathing, downward-facing **yogi.** Wear yoga pants and a tank top emblazoned with a Buddhist saying or depicting a Hindu god. Go barefoot, carry a rolled-up yoga mat, and take on various poses throughout the night. Or just sit quietly in the lotus position (Indian-style, with each foot tucked up on the opposite thigh).

Om. Marisa finds her balance in tree pose.

CHAPTER NINE

Crowd Participation

For the people-person eager to mingle, here's a list of ideas that will let you work the crowd. Get others in the act with these audience-required costumes.

QUIZ SHOW
page 174

SNACK BAR
page 175

FREE PUPPIES TO A GOOD HOME
page 173

BARTENDER

Is there a more effective way to draw a crowd? If you want to be the center of the action this Halloween, make up a pitcher of your favorite cocktail and serve it to all your pals. It's at least worth a shot. Wear black pants, a white button-down shirt, and a vest (ideally black-and-red striped). Add a "Tell me about your life" pin and you're ready to serve.

CIGARETTE GIRL

If Philip Morris had a daughter, no doubt she'd be getting dolled up in this smoking little costume. Throw on a little black dress, a pillbox hat, and some heels. Now take a shallow, rectangular cardboard box (like a soda-can case) and paint it red (or cover it in red wrapping paper, if that's easier). Make a strap (long enough to go around your neck and attach to both sides of the box) out of duct tape by putting the sticky sides of two lengths together. Use more duct tape to attach your strap to the box. Now fill 'er up with cigarettes (emptied from their boxes); use real or candy, depending on your friends' preferences.

KISSING BOOTH

Looking for some action? For this costume, you'll be wearing a large cardboard box. Cut the four flaps from the open side of the box, and save one of the two longer flaps. Turn the box upside down and cut a square out of the side where your face will be. Cut two 2-inch strips from the flap you saved. Duct tape these straps to the front and back inner walls to hang over your arms in an arch. Use a marker to write **"Kissing Booth"** on the top of the cutout area. Then work the crowd.

FREE PUPPIES TO A GOOD HOME

Want to stop traffic this Halloween? Well, who can pass by a box of pups without stopping for a peek? Dress up as a dog: all brown, with floppy ears, a pink nose, a tail, and a collar. Wear brown, white, or tan mittens for paws. Next, out of an open box, cut a hole in the bottom large enough for your waist. Attach two suspenderlike straps made out of duct tape to the box so that you can carry it without hands. On the outside of the box, write "Puppies for Adoption" or "Free Puppies." On the inside, line the bottom with newspaper, and throw in as many plush pups as you can fit.

QUIZ SHOW

Put your pals on the spot by going as a walking **quiz show.** Here's how: Make a sandwich board out of two pieces of cardboard or poster board. On each sheet, cover the outward facing side with categories of personal questions that your friends should know (''My Favorite Foods,'' ''Places I've Lived,'' for example). Then, under each category, draw columns of boxes with ascending values. When someone picks a category and a value, read a statement from a separate prepared sheet of paper. Wait for his or her response (phrased as a question). Carry a buzzer and have lots of candy to give away as prizes.

Sandwich Board Step-by-Step

Making a sandwich board is quick and easy. Choose the material you'll use for your boards (poster board or cardboard are both inexpensive and light). Hold one sheet up to your chest and mark in pencil where the strings should lie across your shoulders. Use pieces of masking or packing tape (affixed to the inside of the board—the side that won't be visible once you're wearing it) to make the board sturdier at the points where you're going to punch the holes (an inch or two from the top of the board). If you don't have a hole punch, put a cutting board under the poster or cardboard (so you don't cut your table or floor), and use an X-Acto knife or scissors to punch the holes. The first board should be used as a guide for the second (put them together as though you're already wearing them—the parts that won't be visible should be facing each other). Use string, twine, ribbon, or clothesline to tie the boards together. The heaviness of the boards you've chosen will dictate the type of string you'll need to use. The strings should be long enough that they can lie directly on your shoulders.

SANTA CLAUS

Our friend Maja was very pleased with her **Santa** costume. "I wore the classic red hat, a white fluffy beard, a heinous Christmas sweat suit that my [name of relative withheld] gave me, and—to make Santa hip to the hip-hop—a studded punk belt to hold up the pillow in my shirt. I had a goody bag filled with tons of candy, small Hanes tighty-whiteys, and huge grandma undies. I distributed all of these gifts to my friends. Santa was a huge hit that year."

SNACK BAR

Use clear packing tape to attach snack-size bags of pretzels, candy, trail mix, and cookies to your clothing. Allow your friends to partake of your **snack bar.** Everyone will be looking at your costume with hungry eyes. Charge reasonable prices.

Animalistic Tendencies

Nothing is more guaranteed to please and pull in a crowd than a costume that includes a pet. Here are some ideas that feature furry and feathery friends.

1. **Dorothy** with **Toto,** a cairn terrier, in a picnic basket

2. **Nurse** or **Doctor** with a **puppy** wrapped in a soft blanket (a **sick puppy**)

3. **Witch** with a **black cat**

4. **Magician** with a **bunny**

5. **Safari guide** with a **snake** (or any kind of slithery creature)

6. **Pirate** with a **parrot**

7. **Princess** with her prince, who's been turned into a **frog.** (No frog? Then bring your dog and blame the witch's unclear pronunciation while spell casting.)

8. **Fireman** with a trusty **dalmatian**

9. **Orphan Annie** and her mutt, **Sandy**

10. **Timmy** and his collie, **Lassie**

11. **Peter** and the **Wolf** (substitute a German shepherd)

12. **Little Red Riding Hood** and the **Wolf** (ditto)

13. **Elle Woods** and her Chihuahua, **Bruiser,** from *Legally Blonde*

14. **Dr. Evil** and his fluffy white cat, **Mr. Bigglesworth** (prior to being cryogenically frozen), from *Austin Powers*

15. **Martin Crane,** Frasier's dad—with a walker and a flannel shirt—and his Jack Russell terrier, **Eddie**

Ashley plays vet to a plush poodle.

CHAPTER TEN

Around the World

GOBLINS
page 181

MARDI GRAS REVELER
page 182

Think globally, trick-or-treat locally! Open your foreign policy and consider these geographically inspired costumes.

CHICAGO
page 179

AN OVERWHELMED TOURIST
page 185

Road Trip: Salem, Massachusetts

It's worth making a pilgrimage to Salem, Massachusetts, just twenty miles north of Boston. Don't miss cultural hot spots such as the newly renovated **Peabody Essex Museum,** which houses three centuries of New England art and architecture, as well as a rich collection of Asian art, and Nathaniel Hawthorne's **House of Seven Gables,** the early nineteenth-century manse that inspired his novel of the same name. At the **Salem Witch Museum,** reenactments of the major moments of this episode in history are staged several times a day in an amphitheater. The life-size "actors" are automated, but the drama carries through.

BOSTON BAKED BEAN

No, you don't have to go as a gooey brown blob (although brown long-sleeved T-shirt and pants are a good foundation for this costume). All you need are a Boston Red Sox (or Celtics) cap and a short-sleeved Boston T-shirt (a team or tourist T will be perfect). Then roll a fake (and we mean fake!) joint, and try to look fried—you're a **Boston Baked Bean!**

Road Trip: Keene, New Hampshire

For the ultimate jack-o'-lantern experience, visit the **Pumpkin Festival** in Keene, New Hampshire. Every year, they attempt to break their own previously set record in the *Guinness Book of Records* for the most lit pumpkins in one place. On October 31, 2003, the town gathered 28,952 lit jack-o'-lanterns on a large scaffolding structure in the town square known as "Pumpkin Central." Seventy thousand people gathered to enjoy the shops, food, fireworks, and kiddy costume parade, which has over 2,000 marchers. The festival has come a long way since the first one thirteen years ago, when Keene gathered 600 pumpkins. For more information or to see pictures, visit the festival's official Web site at **www.pumpkin festival.com.**

CHICAGO

The Windy City: With hairspray and gel and whatever other goop you can find (see page 98), sculpt hair so that it's standing straight to one side—as if there's a fierce wind blowing it that way. Bend wire to shape an old tie or scarf to look like it's blowing in the same direction (see page 109). Use double-sided tape to stick a sheet of newspaper to the left side of your body (as if it's been blown from the ground and has stuck to you). Carry an inside-out umbrella in one hand. Finally, make sure you're wearing a Cubs, Bears, or University of Chicago T-shirt.

A GEISHA

Make it a memoir-worthy Halloween. Wear a silk kimono (or, if you can't find a kimono, a silk Chinese dress with a mandarin collar), hair in a bun secured with chopsticks, and a pow-dered white face with a streak of red down the center of your lips. (Get two friends to do the same, and giggle behind your fans. You're the **three little maids** of Gilbert and Sullivan's *The Mikado.*)

GREEN CARD

If spending time making an elaborate Halloween costume is a foreign concept, it's easy to turn yourself into a **green card.** Take two pieces of green poster board, fasten them together at one of the longer ends, and hang them over your shoulders like a sandwich board (see page 174). Write in bogus information, like a place of birth from outside the United States, and a current address.

PERMANENT RESIDENT CARD

NAME: Average, Joe

Birthdate: My Birthday
Category: Manly
Sex: YES

Country of Origin
Made in the USA

RESIDENT SINCE:
Birth

C1USA9875459-
3495814<<<<45908GIJ45G0LFRII1
<<<<<<HAHAHAHAAHAHA
R09G8409G098KDF

HERSHEY KISS/ FRENCH KISS

To become a **Hershey Kiss,** wear silver clothing or cover your torso and shoulders with aluminum foil. Add a winter hat covered with foil and attach a small white banner that says "Hershey Kiss" to the top. If you want to be a **French kiss,** add a snazzy beret and a fine, penciled-in mustache. Ooh la la!

Goblins, Goblins, Goblins

When happy-go-lucky gnomes, imps, and leprechauns get together for family reunions, they probably hope this side of the family doesn't show up. Goblins—the uglier and more mischievous relatives of gnomes—are known for their tricky and sometimes evil deeds. According to folklore, goblins originated in France, and spread to the rest of Europe—and eventually the world—through a chasm in the Pyrénées. These grotesque globe-trotters are believed to have lived everywhere from the grottoes of large cities to mossy caves in the woods.

Descriptions of goblins' demeanor vary. In some accounts they play harmless tricks, such as knocking over drinks and dirtying clean houses, while at other times they are described as performing evil deeds harmful to humans. If you don't want a goblin for a houseguest, store away the wine and hide your kiddies—goblins can't resist stealing wine and, sometimes, making off with the children.

Among recent depictions of goblins in the popular media:

■ In the world of J. K. Rowling's young wizard, Harry Potter, goblins run the underground wizard bank in London called Gringotts Bank.

■ In J.R.R. Tolkien's *Lord of the Rings* trilogy, *goblin* is another name for *orc,* the small creatures that infested the Misty and the Grey Mountains in the later Third Age, and who had their capital at Mount Gundabad.

■ David Bowie played the Goblin King in Jim Henson and George Lucas's 1986 film *Labyrinth.*

LEPRECHAUN

Celebrate St. Patty's Day a little early. Get into some mischief as a mythic **leprechaun:** You'll need black buckle shoes, white or green stockings, green shorts and top, and green suspenders. Optional: red mutton chops and a matching wig. Added props: a pot full of gold chocolate coins, or a four-leaf clover cut out of green cardboard to get some luck o' the Irish on your side.

Knock, knock.
Who's there?
Goblin.
Goblin who?
Goblin your candy will make your stomach ache!

MARDI GRAS REVELER

What to do with all that loot you scored at last year's **Mardi Gras?** Pile it on and go as a **reveler:** festive, colorful garb accented by strands of beads, feathered mask (held on a stick), maybe a fool's hat. And for the exhibitionist, let this be your chance to show your stuff (if you know what we mean)!

Road Trip: New Orleans, Louisiana

Do you believe in voodoo? There's no better place to learn about this African polytheistic religion than in New Orleans, and there's no better time than during Halloween. Besides partaking in the legendary parties of the French Quarter and Bourbon Street (which do not, by the way, take place exclusively during Mardi Gras) take a tour of **The New Orleans Historic Voodoo Museum.** Around the end of October, the museum hosts its annual **Halloween Voodoo Rituals,** which are not reenactments, but the real thing. If you wish to contact your ancestors, remember to bring an offering of food or drink. If you'd rather leave the dead in peace, why not take a walking tour of one of the city's **historic cemeteries.** The tombs and vaults of these cemeteries are aboveground because of the marshlike conditions of the region, making a wanderer feel like he's walking among the stone buildings of a dead city. Creepy!

NEW YORK

The city that never sleeps. Can you imagine how exhausting that must be? How much caffeine per capita must be consumed? Kind of makes you want to hop a train to the suburbs, where it's possible to get a solid eight hours nightly. Personify the NYC look by drawing enormous shadows under your eyes, messing up your hair, wearing an I ♥ NEW YORK T-shirt over pj's. Drink coffee, soda, or just carry a box of Vivarin, and wear a Yankees cap or a skyline headband (made out of gray construction paper glued to a head-band). Get a pal to go dressed as **The Big Apple:** brown turtleneck, brown knit hat. Fold a red sheet or large piece of red fabric in half, and cut the sides to resemble a large oval with a flat, folded bottom. Sew up the sides, leaving a hole for your wrist on each side. Then cut two leg holes in the bottom fold. Stuff the fabric "pocket" with bubble wrap or anything light and fluffy. Cut a green hand towel in the shape of a leaf and pin it to your costume at the neck.

Road Trip: New York City!

Every Halloween night, throngs of revelers and spectators converge at dusk on Sixth Avenue to celebrate the holiday Greenwich Village–style. Join them, and you'll witness a parade of the most inventive, bizarre, and colorful costumes imaginable. The **Greenwich Village Halloween Parade,** which travels from Spring Street to 22nd Street, has been a Manhattan staple since the 1970s.

THE STATUE OF LIBERTY

Don't restrict outbursts of patriotic fervor to Thanksgiving and the Fourth of July. Halloween's a perfect holiday to wave the flag and dress as one of our nation's favorite dames. Her look's been around since 1884, but it never loses its timeless *Je ne sais quoi.* Buy a light green sheet and drape it around your body (the most conservative toga you can whip up is the right idea—for toga how-to, see page 11). Next, make seven skinny cones out of light green construction paper. Clip ¼-inch nicks into the base, fold them into tabs, and glue them to a light green construction paper headband. Face and body paint in a matching color are a must. Carry a book and a torch (a flashlight covered in foil).

AN OVERWHELMED TOURIST

Here's a trippy costume: Wander around the party with eyes as big as saucers, mouth agape, multiple cameras around your neck. The basic tourist costume should include khaki shorts and a Hawaiian shirt. Then carry as much destination paraphernalia as you can fit on your person. (A tourist in Paris, for example, should be

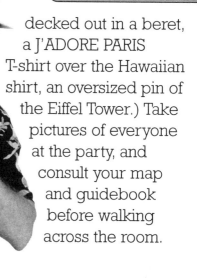

decked out in a beret, a J'ADORE PARIS T-shirt over the Hawaiian shirt, an oversized pin of the Eiffel Tower.) Take pictures of everyone at the party, and consult your map and guidebook before walking across the room.

Halloween Around the World

The **English** largely got off the Halloween track when Martin Luther's Protestant Reformation took hold in the early sixteenth century. Devotees of the new religion didn't believe in saints, a change that rendered All Saints' Day pretty meaningless. But England does have its *own* autumn holiday with bloody origins.

In 1605, notorious British traitor Guy Fawkes was convicted of attempting to blow up England's Parliament building, as part of a larger attempt by a Catholic group to overthrow Protestant King James. Fawkes was executed on November 5, and a celebration of fireworks

King James encouraged the celebration of Guy Fawkes Day to prevent the commoners from feeling that they'd lost out on their old celebrations involving bonfires and the afterworld.) Children wander

and burning effigies ensued immediately. A tradition was born: **Guy Fawkes Day** is still celebrated on November 5 with fireworks launched and bonfires lit throughout England. (Some speculate that

the streets carrying an effigy of Fawkes and ask passersby for "a penny for the guy"— spare change which they get to pocket. Minus the sugar rush, it's the closest thing the

English have to American trick-or-treating.

El Dia de los Muertos (Day of the Dead), celebrated in **Mexico, Spain,** and **Latin America,** is a three-day festival to honor deceased loved ones, who are believed to return to the mortal world during this time. Many cele-brants of *el Dia de los Muertos* welcome the dead by prepar-ing elaborate altars in their homes, offering treats like candy, favorite foods, flowers, water, and sometimes even a basin and washcloth so the deceased visitor can "freshen up" before indulging in a festive meal. Gravesites are tended and decorated, and on the last day of the holiday, family members often gather at the grave to memorialize the dead and reminisce about the good times.

In **Ireland,** Halloween's ances-tral birthplace, October 31 is celebrated in traditions very similar to those of America. Irish kids get dressed up in costumes and go trick-or-treating for candy in their neighborhoods. There's also a strong tie to the ancient idea that Halloween is a day for predicting the future. Barmbrack (see page 212) is a traditional Irish Halloween food, similar to fruitcake, inside which several goodies are baked. According to tradition, these goodies give their recipients clues about the year to come. For example, the person who finds the ring inside the cake will soon tie the knot; if you find yourself biting into a thimble, on the other hand, spinsterhood is your future.

THE U.N.

Simply stick lots of miniflags all over your clothing. You can buy nylon or sticker miniflags at a flag store or from a Web site like **www.unflags.com.** Or if you have a color printer, you can print your own from a Web site like **www.worldpeace.org** (click on Flags of All Nations).

Road Trip: San Francisco, California

San Francisco has one of the largest impromptu Halloween to-do's in the country. Like a huge neighborhood party, locals and tourists alike gather in the tiny streets of the Castro wearing masks, costumes, or sometimes (although we don't recommend it) close to nothing! The city cops maintain the crowd and block off traffic as the goblins, drag queens, ladybugs, nuns, and . . . you name it, mingle together in celebration of the spooky holiday. A tamer party is held at the city's Civic Center for children. There is an admission fee, but food and planned events are included.

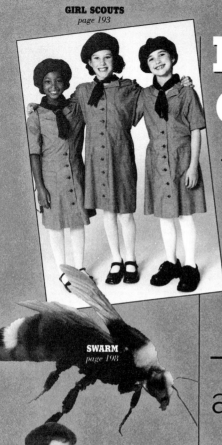

GIRL SCOUTS
page 193

CHAPTER ELEVEN

GIRL SCOUTS
page 193

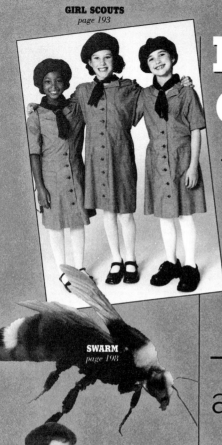

CRAYON
page 190

For the Group

Why traipse around solo as a Halloween loner when you can make your costume —and the holiday— all about having a great time with friends instead? With these fun ideas, the more, the merrier!

SWARM
page 198

PLAYING CARDS
page 195

CRAYOLA

CRAYONS
(UNLIMITED NUMBER)

Stay between the lines with your pals this Halloween—get everyone to dress up as a different color **crayon** in the Crayola spectrum! The costume's easier than it might seem. Make a cylinder out of poster board (see page 26) designed to look like a crayon, using a black marker (you can write the name of the color or "Crayola," but just make sure everyone else does the same). Slide into the cylinder from the bottom up, so that the cylinder hangs from chest height, but underneath your arms. Then make a pointy hat out of the same color. Everyone carries a coloring book.

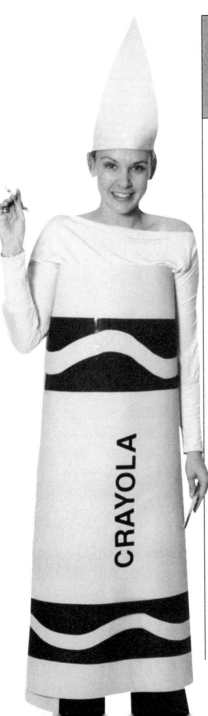

AN EPIDEMIC
(UNLIMITED NUMBER)

Get your gang to wear pajamas and slippers, cover their faces, arms, and any visible skin in distinct-looking red bumps or splotches. Travel in a pack. Pretend to sneeze on anyone who comes near you. Add a nurse or a doctor if you want to keep your **epidemic** under control.

Q: Why are graveyards so noisy?
A: There's so much coffin.

GANGRENE
(UNLIMITED NUMBER)

For this one, everyone wears all-green attire with gobs of green face paint on all exposed skin. Voilà! You've transformed yourselves into **"gangrene"** (Get it? Gang green?) and you're ready to paint the town red. (This costume, incidentally, can evolve in useful ways as the night progresses. A tall individualist, for example, can put on a happier face and become the **Jolly Green Giant.** And any overaggressive late-night behavior can be blamed on the **Incredible Hulk.**)

GIRL SCOUTS
(UNLIMITED NUMBER)

Got a troop of girlfriends with whom you'd like to go trick-or-treating? Earn your friendship patch as **Girl Scouts:** The uniform is khaki pants or skirts, white or light blue button-down shirts, and khaki-colored sashes. Add homemade pins and merit badges for all the skills you've mastered: "Procrastinating at work," "Talking on the phone," "Gossiping." The same idea goes for **Boy Scouts,** dressed in tan shirts and brown pants, carrying canteens and compasses.

GROUPIES
(UNLIMITED NUMBER)

Gather your favorite girls, choose your collective favorite rock band, and make yourselves into the worst kind of **groupies.** You'll need to make T-shirts proclaiming your love for the lead singer/guitarist/drummer of chosen band. Then cover yourselves in band paraphernalia, make posters offering to bear band members' children, and top the whole thing off with pounds of glittery makeup and teeny-bopper accessories.

Glitter: A Cautionary Tale

The expression "too much of a good thing" might have been coined with glitter in mind. Exercise restraint when adding that extra glow to your **sugar-plum fairy,** your **Tinkerbell,** or your twinkling **star.** Otherwise, you'll be picking it out of your carpet, as well as any item of furniture and clothing that comes within a one-mile radius for years to come.

Rent the movie Rock Star to see Jennifer Aniston's take on being a groupie.

PLAYING CARDS
(UP TO 52)

Choose your favorite suit and make a giant playing card, using a piece of large white poster board. Draw a simple design on another piece of poster board to wear as the back of a playing card. Wear them together as a sandwich board (see page 174), with the card face in front and the design on your back. Make similar placards for a pack of your friends—perhaps even going as a royal flush.

THE PRESIDENT OF THE UNITED STATES AND HIS SECRET SERVICE (UNLIMITED NUMBER)

Here's a good one for a pack of guys. One of you will caricature the current president (or just imitate his look and mannerisms), possibly using a mask or just looking tidy and conservative. The rest of the group wears black or navy blue suits and shades, and uses either headset phones or walkie-talkies.

A SIX PACK
(FOR SIX PEOPLE)

Here's another fun one for a group, provided everyone's of legal age! Mimic the design of your favorite beer (or soda) on a piece of poster board, and make a cylinder (see page 26). Wrap a baseball cap with aluminum foil to become the pull tab. If you can rope five friends into doing the same thing, you're a traveling **six pack!**

A SWARM
(UNLIMITED NUMBER)

Here's an idea that's sure to generate some buzz. Get a group of friends to dress up as bees, and go out as a **swarm!** The basic costume: tight black leggings, with a yellow-and-black-striped T-shirt on top. If you can't find a striped shirt, use a black one and create stripes with yellow duct tape. Add some wings (see page 5) and antennae, and appoint one of the girls to be the "queen" by adding a tiara to her costume. See Queen Bee, page 42, for more specifics.

Party Planning

Precious little can top the joy of trick-or-treating your way to a large candy crop . . . but for variety's sake, consider throwing a well-planned Halloween party this year. All your pals + inventive costumes + fun decor + the Halloween spirit = a night you'll all remember.

THE DRINKS MENU

Make the 31st warm and fuzzy by working towards a little buzzy! Here are a few **drinkable** concoctions that you and your guests will appreciate:

BLOODY MARY

I want to suck your . . . Bloody Mary!

- **1½ ounces vodka**
- **3 ounces tomato juice**
- **squeeze of lemon**
- **½ teaspoon horseradish**
- **dash Worcestershire sauce**
- **dash Tabasco sauce**
- **shake of pepper**

Combine in a glass with ice. Stir gently. Garnish with a stalk of celery.

ZOMBIE

Drink more than one, and you'll feel like a zombie.

- **2 shots light rum**
- **1 shot dark rum**
- **1 shot pineapple juice**
- **1 shot lime juice**
- **1 teaspoon powdered sugar**
- **dash 151-proof rum for the top**

Shake the first five ingredients with crushed ice. Strain into a glass filled with ice. Gently pour the 151-proof rum on top. Garnish with a cherry.

ALL HALLOW'S EVE MARTINI

The perfect orange drink for Halloween sophisticates.

- **1½ ounces vodka**
- **1 ounce Grand Marnier**
- **splash orange curaçao**

Combine in a shaker. Serve chilled.

PUMPKIN EATER

Peter, Peter should have served his wife this yummy concoction.

- **1½ ounces light rum**
- **1 ounce orange curaçao**
- **½ ounce triple sec**
- **1 ounce orange juice**
- **½ ounce cream**

Combine ingredients with ice in a blender.

HALLOWEEN SCHNAPPS

Here's a seasonal drink with snap!

- **1 part apple schnapps**
- **1 part cinnamon schnapps**

Mix equal amounts of each schnapps in shot glasses.

SQUIRMY-WORMIES: A.K.A. JELL-O SHOTS

They're *aliiive!!*

Buy some orange or blackberry Jell-O and follow directions on the back of the box, pouring the mixture into a shallow pan. If you want to spice it up, add a few splashes of vodka to the water. Cut the Jell-O into shapes using Halloween cookie cutters and place them on a platter. Keep refrigerated until ready to serve.

BODY PART SANGRIA

After a few of these, your guests might really start to believe the fruits are eyeballs, fingers, and toes.

- **1 bottle dry red wine**
- **1 cup orange juice**
- **¼ cup white sugar**
- **1 lemon, sliced**
- **1 lime, sliced**
- **1 cup seedless green grapes**
- **1 cup pineapple chunks**
- **1 apple, sliced**
- **1 liter carbonated soda**

In a large pitcher, combine the ingredients, minus the carbonated soda, stirring well. Refrigerate and allow the mixture to sit for as long as possible (two hours to overnight). When ready to serve, add the carbonated soda and mix well.

STRAIGHT BLOOD: A.K.A. RED WINE

No secret here . . . red wine is the perfect potion on a cool autumn night. All you've got to do to make it appropriately ghoulish is cover the label on your wine bottles with labels marked "Blood Type O+," "Blood Type A–," and so on. Offer your guests a transfusion.

MAULED CIDER

Those braving the cold can stay toasty with this spiced concoction.

- **20 cloves**
- **5 apples**
- **1 gallon apple cider**
- **2 or 3 cinnamon sticks**
- **zest of 1 orange**
- **2 or 3 cups rum (optional)**

Push 4 cloves into each apple and put them in a large pot. Pour the apple cider into the pot, drop a few cinnamon sticks in, and zest the orange directly over it. Warm the brew over medium-low heat, but don't let it boil. Leave it on the stove for about an hour and a half. Add rum to your liking, or add a shot to each glass just before serving. Drink up while it's still warm.

Offer your teetotaling guests some **Virgin Sacrifices:** orange soda, Coke, or Pepsi. Add an orange slice for an accent to keep with the Halloween-color theme.

THE BUFFET TABLE

Here's a grocery list of black and orange foods to get your creative juices flowing . . . festive, with very little culinary talent or time investment required. (For additional recipes, see page 210.)

ORANGE TREATS

- **Grilled cheese sandwiches made with orange cheddar or American cheese**
- **Macaroni and cheese**
- **Cheese dip (best with blue tortilla chips)**
- **Carrots**
- **Orange peppers**
- **Doritos**
- **Cheetos**
- **American, cheddar, Munster cheese**
- **Cheese Nips**
- **Orange-flavored Jell-O**
- **Oranges, tangerines, clementines, cantaloupe**
- **Carrot cake**

BLACK (OR DARK BROWN) TREATS

- **Olives**
- **Black bean dip**
- **Blue tortilla chips**
- **Caviar**
- **Pumpernickel bread**
- **Prunes, figs, raisins**
- **Licorice bits**
- **Brownies**
- **Black Forest cake**

HUMAN BODY PARTS

Make little signs for each of these, so your guests know what they are.

- **Loose grapes (eyeballs)**
- **Spareribs from your local Chinese restaurant (human ribs)**
- **Dried apricots (preserved ears)**

RALLYING YOUR TROOPS

Looking to transform this year's Halloween celebration into a distinct and memorable experience? Why not create a theme for your party? Ask your guests to dress for the occasion, and then decorate accordingly. It takes a little extra planning and effort, but the results are guaranteed to add some energy to your night.

ROCK STARS

Q: What do you get when you throw Ozzy Osborne in a room with Pink and Jimi Hendrix?
A: A pretty unbeatable party and a nomination to the Hostess Hall of Fame. Add a dj to the mix and instruct him to play the musical hits of your attendees. Or, really go for the gold, and rent a karaoke machine.

Encourage your guests to give live performances, and hold a mock Grammy Awards ceremony at the end of the night. The party invitations should look like rock concert tickets, and your front door or hallway should have a red carpet rolled out. Rock on!

THE WILD WEST

Cowboys and cowgirls, circle your wagons! Ask your guests to bust out their finest ten-gallon hats, spurs, denim, bandannas, and leather. Make a "campfire" in the fireplace and hang some homemade WANTED posters with photos of your guests. Serve chili. Put out some bales of hay and play some twangy country music. Set up a saloon where your thirsty cowhands can drink and play cards. Stage a dramatic pistol duel (with fake guns, of course), and let your guests judge who "shot first."

TARTS AND VICARS

Oh, behave! Follow through on the party that Bridget Jones *almost* went to. Get your crew to dress up as clergymen or ladies of the night, and you're sure to get everyone hot under the collar! Serve red wine and tarts.

LITERARY CHARACTERS

Take a page from your favorite book
And celebrate Halloween with a
literary look.

> *Where: Our library*
> *When: October 31st*

Exude a bookish charm by inviting your guests to dress as a fictional character from their favorite book. Or, if they prefer, have them dress as their favorite author. Everyone—Alice in Wonderland, Virginia Woolf, Madame Bovary, Hunter S. Thompson, and Odysseus—will show up.

JAMES BOND CHARACTERS

Your mission, should you choose to accept it, is to host a 007 bash where your friends dress the part of James Bond, his many sexy conquests, and his evil enemies. Rent 007 movies and play them. Or, if you can, project them onto the walls as background scenery. Play sultry international music or invest in the sound tracks of the Bond movies. Serve martinis . . . shaken, not stirred.

PIRATES

Thar she blows! Assemble all your best mates for some high-seas adventure, and hoist the skull and crossbones over your front door. Pull out the tattered clothing, gold hoop earrings, eye patches, and lay the

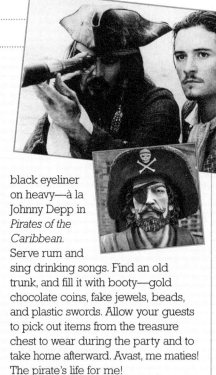

black eyeliner on heavy—à la Johnny Depp in *Pirates of the Caribbean.* Serve rum and sing drinking songs. Find an old trunk, and fill it with booty—gold chocolate coins, fake jewels, beads, and plastic swords. Allow your guests to pick out items from the treasure chest to wear during the party and to take home afterward. Avast, me maties! The pirate's life for me!

COME AS YOU AREN'T

Invite everyone to dress as his or her polar opposite. Your super conservative friend can come as a freewheeling hippie; a notorious flirt can dress as a nun; manly guys come dolled up as girls; a confident, independent gal can be a doormat for the evening. Couples could come as opposites: light and dark, comedy and tragedy, hot and cold. Decorate your place with yin-yang symbols.

HOSTED BY CUPID

Don't reserve your matchmaking skills for Valentine's Day. If you don't think your friends will mind too much having their costumes dictated by you, play love puppeteer: Match up your guest list in pairs, and assign each person as half of a pair on his or her invitation. For example, invite Single Friend #1 to be Tarzan/Bert/Pat Sajak and Single Friend #2 to be Jane/Ernie/Vanna White . . . When they arrive, let them find their mate! Your guests might feel temporarily awkward, but will have *something* in common: blaming you. (If your friends are already coupled off, give them a little room to be creative, as long as their costumes are paired as well.)

A CREEPY CRAWL

Don't feel like hosting all night? Recruit a few volunteers and devise a "creepy crawl," in which guests go treat-seeking from house to house (or in our case, apartment to apartment). Each stop in the progressive dinner should provide a unique food and drink—stops could include appetizer, soup, salad, main dish, and dessert courses. At the end of this lineup, guests will be crawling their way home. (Suggestion: If nobody is eager to be the designated driver, splurge on hiring a van and driver to carry you around for the night—a reasonable expense if split many ways.)

CHAPTER TWELVE

A Movable Feast

CORN ON
THE COB
page 205

With the deluge of candy on Halloween, is it any wonder we all have food on the brain? Here are some yummy ideas to wear.

SPAGHETTIOS
page 208

PIG IN A BLANKET
page 208

BAG OF JELLY BEANS/ GUMBALL MACHINE

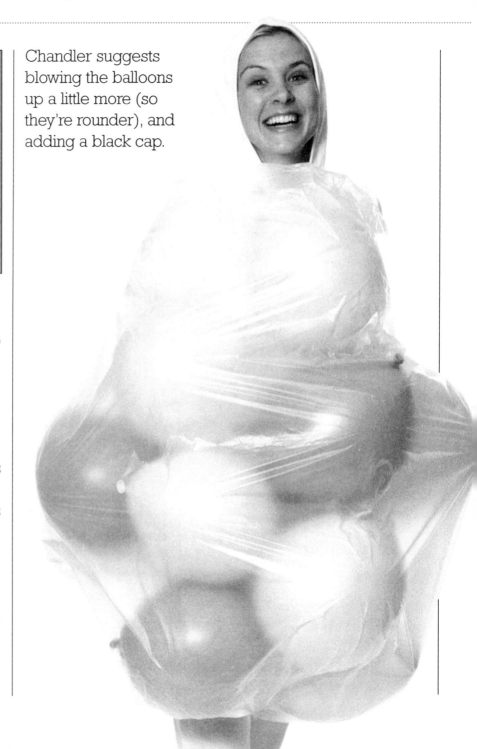

Fill an enormous, clear trash bag with half blown-up balloons. Make two holes at the bottom and two at the sides that are just big enough for your legs and arms to fit through. You don't want to lose balloons during the night, so keep the holes tight to your legs and arms by taping them to your pants and sleeves with clear tape. Also tape the opening of the trash bag at your shoulders, and you're a **bag of jelly beans.** To become a **gumball machine,** our friend Chandler suggests blowing the balloons up a little more (so they're rounder), and adding a black cap.

BUNCH OF GRAPES

Dress all in purple and pin purple balloons all over yourself. Add a purple cap topped off with a green pipe cleaner bent into a curlicue.

CORN ON THE COB

Here's one you can sink your teeth into. Buy enough bubble wrap (the large-size bubbles look best) to wrap around your entire body. Spray paint the bubble side yellow and let it dry. Wrap the bubble wrap around your body and tape it shut with yellow duct or clear packing tape. There are a couple of routes you can go with your hair. Temporarily dye it green to become the cob's stalk. Or pop on a light green or yellow cap—or top off the cob with a piece of leftover painted bubble wrap. Your costume is sure to get lots of compliments—unless your friends are just trying to butter you up.

MILK AND COOKIES

Hungry for a satisfying costume? Get one friend to dress as a carton of milk (large white cardboard box with a cardboard peak, the word *milk* and a picture of a cow on the side). Everyone else constructs circle-shaped sandwich boards (see page 174) out of thick brown cardboard and colors them in with big dark brown dots.

OREO COOKIE

Our friend Marisa recalls her favorite costume, circa eighth grade. Her two best friends dressed all in black, and she dressed all in white. After ringing neighbors' doorbells, the three girls would smush themselves together as close as they possibly could. Between peals of giggles, someone managed to explain that they were an **Oreo cookie.** Absolutely smashing!

PEPPERMINT STICK

Get caught up in red tape! Buy some red duct or electrical tape at your local hardware store. Dress all in white, and wrap the tape in diagonal stripes up your body. To go the extra step, paint your face white, and add a diagonal streak of red. Pull your hair up and put it under a red or white hat.

PICNIC

Who doesn't love dining al fresco? Turn yourself into a **picnic** by stepping into an unconstructed cardboard box. Stand in one corner and fold down two adjacent flaps so that they wedge you in (cut the other two flaps off). Cut a disposable red-and-white checked tablecloth so that it covers the box and can be closed behind you. To hold the "table" up, punch a hole in each of the front corners, knot a ribbon on one end, thread through one hole, run it around your neck and through the other hole. Knot that end. Glue your favorite picnic items to the top of the table.

Draw an army of ants marching up one side of the cloth.

PIG IN A BLANKET

Pig out without guilt! Dress all in pink, paint your face to match, add a pink pipe cleaner curlicue tail, and two little piggy ears and a snout (store-bought probably works best). Now wrap yourself up in a cuddly lap blanket.

SPAGHETTIOS

Cut beige doughnut shapes out of felt and glue them onto a red sweat suit. Paint your face red with a beige *O* around one eye. You're the inside of a bowl of **SpaghettiOs.**

TEA BAG

Do you often find yourself in hot water? Then this costume will suit you to a T: Take one large piece of sheer white fabric about double the length of your torso. Fold it in half and cut a generous hole in the center for your head to fit through. Then sew up the sides and some of the bottom of your square (you need room enough for your torso to fit through). Once you have it on, ask a friend to sew (or glue or staple) up the rest of the bottom so it's as tight to your body as possible. Fill via the neck opening with dried and crushed leaves or a reasonable facsimile (ripped up green/brown paper will do). Attach a piece of string with an oversized tea bag tag to the top.

Q: Where do baby ghosts go during the day?
A: A dayscare center.

Halloween Recipes

Here is a collection of snack ideas that range from the nostalgic to the ghoulish.

SAND-WITCHES

Sandwiches always make good party food, and they're a snap to make. Choose your favorite filling, but we love PB&F—an elementary school classic also known as the Fluffernutter. Most of us haven't eaten these since childhood, but Halloween seems like the perfect time to resurrect these delicious treats. Use white bread, creamy peanut butter, and Fluff to make multiple sandwiches. Then, using Halloween cookie cutters, turn these basic sandwiches into ghostly treats. Or if you don't have any cutters on hand, trim the sides and the top to make a coffin-shaped hexagon. Of course, you can use the same idea with any kind of sandwich you fancy.

MEAT AND VEGETABLE VERTEBRAE

These vertebrae can form the backbone of a great buffet.

8 8-inch flour tortillas

2 8-ounce packages of softened cream cheese

sun-dried tomatoes

4 cups fresh baby spinach leaves

12 ounces thinly sliced deli meat, like salami or prosciutto

Spread the tortillas with the cream cheese, and layer with the tomatoes, spinach leaves, and deli meats. Roll 'em up, cut off the ends, and slice them into inch-wide pieces. Lay them in spine-length rows.

LITTLE TOES

Little toes make great finger food.

Vienna sausages

whole-wheat tortillas

ketchup

Heat the oven to 350°F. Cut a little corner out of the end of each wiener in the shape of a little toe-nail. Cut the tortillas in ⅛-inch-wide strips. Roll each wiener up in a strip and hold it together with a toothpick. Bake for 7 to 8 minutes. Fill each toenail with ketchup. Take toothpicks out before serving.

A perfect blood look-alike

IGA
Tomato
KETCHUP
Rich and Thick
NET WT 24 OZ (1 LB 8 OZ) 680 g

EYEBALL SOUP

Set out a cauldron of melon puree with peeled seedless grapes. Add sugar to taste.

GROWLING CANDY-CORN BARK

This confection is so tasty, everyone will growl for more.

16 Halloween Oreo cookies (in orange and black), coarsely chopped

1½ cups of mini pretzel twists, coarsely broken

⅓ cup raisins

12 ounces chocolate chips

⅓ cup candy corn

2 tablespoons brown and orange sprinkles

Spread cookies, pretzels, and raisins into a 13" x 9" rectangle on a lightly greased sheet. Melt chocolate in a small saucepan on

Vampire fangs

a low flame, stirring constantly. Then drizzle the chocolate over the cookie mixture, using a spatula to make sure it's evenly spread. Add candy corn and colored sprinkles to top, lightly pressing into the mixture so they stick. Allow to cool, and then break into pieces. This takes about 15 minutes to make, and you'll have almost 2 pounds of bark. Store in a festive tin. This also makes a great host/hostess gift.

WITCHES' HATS

Here are some basic instructions for this yummy Halloween treat. But feel free to get creative! Decorate your cone-caps with your own designs. No matter how they look, you know they'll taste great.

box of 12 chocolate ice cream cones

12 3-inch chocolate cookies

orange and black M&M's

candy corn

chocolate frosting

Fill each cone with little candies. Use a plastic bag with one corner snipped off to put icing on the edge of the cone. Put cookie on the top of the cone (or base of the hat) and place on waxed paper. Decorate as you please.

SOUL CAKES

Remember these, the original Halloween treats? If not, go back to page viii.

2 sticks butter

3¾ cups sifted flour

1 cup sugar

1½ teaspoons cinnamon

1 teaspoon ginger

¼ teaspoon allspice

½ teaspoon nutmeg

2 eggs

2 teaspoons cider vinegar

powdered sugar

1. Preheat the oven to 350°F.

2. Cut the butter into the flour with a fork.

3. Add the sugar, cinnamon, ginger, allspice, and nutmeg.

4. Beat the eggs in a separate bowl, then add the vinegar to the eggs.

5. Add the egg mixture to the flour mixture and beat until a stiff dough forms.

6. Knead and roll out, about a ¼-inch thick. Use the lip of a drinking glass to cut the dough into rounds and set them on a greased baking sheet.

7. Prick the top of the cakes with a fork. Bake for 20 to 25 minutes.

8. Let them cool and then sprinkle with powdered sugar.

PUMPKIN BREAD

The cloves give this tasty Halloween treat a spicy flavor—delicious for a snack, or even a light dessert. Serve the bread warm with butter or a little dab of whipped cream.

> **1 cup packed brown sugar**
>
> **⅓ cup shortening**
>
> **2 eggs**
>
> **1 cup canned pumpkin**
>
> **¼ cup milk**
>
> **2 cups flour**
>
> **2 teaspoons baking powder**
>
> **½ teaspoon salt**
>
> **¼ teaspoon baking soda**
>
> **1 teaspoon cloves**
>
> **½ cup walnuts, chopped**
>
> **½ cup raisins**

1. Preheat the oven to 350°F and grease a loaf pan with butter.

2. Mix together the brown sugar and shortening. Mix in the eggs and add the canned pumpkin and milk. Blend until smooth.

3. In a separate bowl, mix together the flour, baking powder, salt, baking soda, and cloves.

4. Add the two mixtures together (flour and pumpkin) and stir well, adding the nuts and raisins.

5. Pour batter into the buttered pan, and bake for 55 minutes, or until a knife comes out clean. After it's done, allow the bread to cool for ten minutes, then remove it from the pan, and cool on a rack.

BARMBRACK

An age-old Irish tradition, kids and adults love this cake for its great taste and the trinkets they'll find inside. Use fun, heat-resistant trinkets to wrap in foil and add to the batter—rings, coins, and figurines usually do the trick. Warn guests not to swallow the goodies.

> **2¾ cups dried mixed fruit (apricots, figs, dates, raisins, and cherries)**
>
> **1 cup of Irish tea**
>
> **¾ cup sugar**
>
> **1 egg**
>
> **4 cups flour**
>
> **1 teaspoon baking powder**
>
> **1 teaspoon of mixed spices: two parts cinnamon to one part ginger and one part cloves**

1. Preheat oven to 350°F.

2. Allow the dried fruit to soak in the tea overnight. The following day, add the sugar and egg to the fruit mix, then sift in the flour, baking powder, and spices. Mix

the dough gently in order to avoid breaking up the fruit.

3. Stir your trinkets gently into the dough.

4. Bake in an 8" round pan for about 65 or 70 minutes, or until a toothpick comes out clean. Turn out and cool on a wire rack. Serve with butter and a cup of Irish tea.

DIRT AND WORMS PIE

Looks disgusting, tastes delicious!

> **1 3.4 oz. box of instant chocolate pudding**
>
> **2 cups milk**
>
> **prepared graham cracker pie crust (9-inch)**
>
> **gummy worms**
>
> **box of chocolate cookies or Oreo cookies, crushed**

Prepare the pudding as directed. Pour it into the pie crust, along with the gummy worms, making sure that some are sticking out of the "ground." Sprinkle a thick layer of chocolate cookies over the pie, again making sure that some parts of the worms are visible.

CHAPTER THIRTEEN

Odds and Ends

Not sure whether you're looking for sexy sizzle, historical heritage, or sporty spice? You don't have to choose. Some of the best costumes defy simple categorization.

LUCKY CHARM
page 223

SCOTCH AND SODA
page 227

USED-CAR SALESMAN
page 233

MONTH OF MARCH
page 225

BUTLER
page 216

ACCIDENT PRONE

Got two left feet? Lost a few teeth to Mr. Sidewalk? Do black cats see you coming and run the other way? This is the costume for you. Embrace your klutziness, and be **accident prone** this Halloween: Put an arm in a sling; give yourself a black eye (see page 28); wrap an Ace bandage around one ankle and use gauze to make a cast on the other leg; see if you can dig up someone's old neck brace; hobble around on crutches; black out a few teeth, wrap gauze around your head to bandage a forehead wound.

BARBIE AND KEN

To step out as that plastic-perfect couple (recent divorce notwithstanding), **Barbie** needs a wild print '70s halter dress or fuchsia and lime bell-bottoms and T-shirt outfit, long blond hair, lots of makeup, and stilettos. Her blander male counterpart, **Ken,** wears dorky short-sleeved shirt and trousers, and side-parted, immovable hair. (Go online or to any toy store for inspiration.) Fake tans for both. Walk stiffly and don't bend your arms.

Then there are endless variations. We like **House-wife Ken** and **Wall Street Barbie.** He's in blue pants, a white shirt, frilly white apron, with a feather duster, and she's in a sexy pin-striped skirt suit, glasses, with a briefcase.

BELLY BUTTON LINT

Aaah, the wonders of the white sweat suit! Turn yours inside out to become the mysterious clump of fibers that seems to suddenly and magically appear in belly buttons all over the world.

BRIDEZILLA

Make amends for past real-life **Bridezilla** behavior by letting your friends laugh at you. Wear a white formal dress, devil horns, and green makeup on your face, arms, and hands. They'll know who you are as soon as they see you.

BUTLER

Wear a tux with tails (you might have to hit a few thrift stores for this), slick down your hair, carry a silver tray, and pronounce in your best English accent, "Will that be all, sir?" and "You rang?" A monocle and white gloves, if you can find them, are excellent touches. (For further inspiration, we suggest a viewing of Robert Altmann's *Gosford Park.*) Carry a feather duster in your back pocket.

COUNTRY CLUB COUPLE

Play a couple of sets or 18 holes before lunch on the club terrace. She wears tennis togs (a skirt is better than shorts) and he wears his golf outfit, complete with argyle socks and tassled shoes. Speak with fake lockjaw, telling friends, "So splendid to see you."

DEBUTANTE

Why not poke a little fun at the **debutante** scene? Poofy white dress (with puffed sleeves and bows if you can find it— it's more fun to go with a touch of the '80s), a bouquet of red roses in one hand, a half-empty bottle of Tanqueray in the other. Bottoms up, sweet-heart!

DEEP-SEA EXPLORER

Got scuba gear? Pull it on and take the plunge. Add some netting around your shoulders, attach some shells and starfish, and carry around a hidden treasure map.

DRY CLEANING

Y ou know those weeks when you don't have time to run errands, let alone come up with an inventive costume? Well, should one of those weeks fall just before Halloween, here's how to kill two birds with one stone: Pick up those clothes that have been at the cleaners for months, and hold on to the plastic and a hanger that says "Fast and Easy Cleaners: We ♥ our customers." Then, wear the plastic like a poncho, and attach the paper from the hanger to your neck so that it's readable.

FASHION VICTIM

F or every trendsetter who says, "Why not footless tights with a lacy hem?" or "I *love* ruffles," or "Acid wash, yes!" there is a flock of followers who try, and fail, to own the look themselves. Yes, we're talking about the **fashion victim,** the girl who can't say no to a trend. We see you coming a mile away, and we know—judging

by your '70s-style gym shorts paired with bright red 4-inch heels, a velvet jacket plus big frizzy hair, a nameplate necklace, and last year's Fendi baguette knock-off— that you've once again let Sarah Jessica Parker get to your head. For shame. This Halloween, indulge in every bad and unflattering trend that ever was—get it out of your system so we can all move on.

FRAT BRAT

Been a while since you kicked a keg? Relive your glory days, complete with "Co-ed Naked Lacrosse" T-shirt (or something bearing Greek letters, Calvin and Hobbes, or a Budweiser reference), beer goggles (and pitcher to go with), backward baseball cap, lacrosse shorts, and flip-flops. Delta Tau Chi forever!

HEAD ON A SILVER PLATTER

Guess what's for dinner? You are! Buy a large aluminum easy-bake tray. Cut a line from the back of the tray to the center, then cut a circle for your neck. Tape the cut edges of the tray with duct tape and wear a turtleneck, so the aluminum won't scrape your skin. Add some parsley and lettuce as garnish. Cut radishes and carrots to look like roses, and affix them to the platter by sticking tacks through from underneath the platter and covering the bottom with silver duct tape.

HOUSEWIFE

Take a load off, hon. Get yourself some bonbons, slip on your favorite housecoat, throw on your fluffy pink slippers, give yourself a facial, put curlers in your hair, leaf through *Soap Opera Digest,* flip channels with your remote control, and talk on the phone . . . in short, go as the worst possible stereotype of a **housewife.** Oh, and don't forget to carry a dinner plate of burnt meatloaf and instant mashed potatoes. Well, you can't be expected to do *everything*!

HOT-AIR BALLOON

To get this costume off the ground, buy a cheap plastic laundry basket and cut a hole in the bottom large enough for your torso to fit through. Wear two straps like suspenders to keep the basket in place. (Or buy a hip-hugging laundry basket and strap it around your waist.) Tie 10 to 12 helium-filled balloons around your basket. Purists can put the balloons in a see-through garbage bag and attach the bag upside down to the basket.

HUNTER

Let loose your killer instinct. Go camouflage from head to ankle, don hiking or work boots, and add your weapon of choice—bow and arrow, rifle, or bowie knife. A dead animal (a stuffed toy or piece of fur) completes the costume.

INCOGNITO

A bit of a cop out? Perhaps—but if you're going to be lazy about your Halloween costume, at least try not to get recognized. Wear a trench coat, a hat, and dark glasses. Lurk in corners.

JACOB'S LADDER

Take a page from the Good Book. First, dress conservatively. Find or make a rope or paper ladder that runs the length of your body, and drape it over your head or carry it. A nice finishing touch: Add a name tag to your shirt: JACOB.

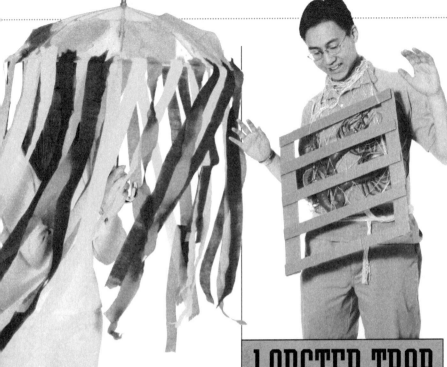

LUCKY CHARM

Feeling lucky? Why take any chances: Cover yourself in rabbits' feet, lucky pennies, and construction paper four-leaf clovers. We suggest trick-or-treating at a casino.

LOBSTER TRAP

First, make part of a **lobster trap** with cardboard "slats." Tangle a few lobsters (homemade or store bought) in some netting. Dress all in blue and wrap the netting around you so that the lobsters are obvious. Tie a string to the lobster trap and hang it around your neck.

JELLYFISH

Float through Halloween this year. Carry a clear umbrella and tape paper streamers along the edges.

LUMBERJACK

Throw on a flannel shirt, construction boots, and overalls, and carry a saw or ax. A beard is a good touch. Don't forget to yell, "Timber!"

MICROPHONE

Project yourself into this simple costume: a rounded cap (a black skullcap works fine), and a radio station's call letters (WKRP, for example) written on a piece of paper and tied as a choker around your neck. Wear all gray or black and keep your arms at your sides. You'll never have so many people asking if you're "turned on."

MONOPOLY MAN

Toss on your finest three-piece suit, a proper top hat, draw or glue on a mustache, and stuff your pockets with lots of fake cash.

MONTH OF MARCH

You've heard the adage about the **month of March:** It "comes in like a lion, goes out like a lamb." Personify the month by costuming the front half of your body as the King of the Jungle, and the back as one of Little Bo Peep's charges. Here's how: Divide your hair into front and back halves. Rat and hairspray the front section to look like a mane. With the back half, tie into a tight bun (or curl into tight, compact curls) and powder white. The outfit: Wear flesh-colored clothing. On your back half, glue cotton balls all over, a few extra balled up to be a stubby tail. On the front, sew on a piece of golden faux fur that goes down to your belly; sew on fur cuffs, too. For your face, paint on whiskers and a black nose (see feline makeup, page 119).

NUN AND PRIEST

Uh-oh . . . We wouldn't make this up ourselves, but we will pass on this very deviant costume idea: a knocked-up **nun** and a **priest.** She'll need a habit (a long-sleeved, long black dress, white fabric wrapped around her face, and black fabric on her head) and a pillow for padding. He'll need black pants, black turtle-neck with a piece of white duct tape at the neck for his clerical collar, and black suit jacket. Carry a rosary or cross.

THE OCEAN

Who isn't captivated by the beauty of the sea? Everyone will admire this simple costume, too. Wear a flowy blue dress, pin on some homemade or plastic fish (add whales, dolphins, or sharks, if you like), slip on seashell jewelry. Make yourself a headpiece out of netting and a lobster, and if you want, use some blue glitter makeup. One look at you and your friends will be able to smell the salt in the air.

Q-TIP

For a hygiene-conscious costume-slacker: Wrap yourself in blue Saran wrap (we don't need to point out that you shouldn't cover your face, do we?), and cover a white hat with double-sided tape and lots and lots of cotton balls.

"Tooth"some Options

Some costumes require a less-than-complete set of teeth. If you currently have all of your choppers, buy a bottle of tooth black, available at any costume or Halloween shop. Dry each tooth you want to black out and then paint the liquid on. Your teeth will be back to their natural color after a regular brushing with toothpaste.

Note: If your costume specifically calls for a redneck look, costume and Halloween shops stock fake teeth in styles like "Bubba," "Billy Bob," or "Cletus."

ROBOT

Our friend Bob is a Halloween fanatic and is also very crafty. He made this **robot** out of cardboard boxes, silver paint, and a plastic bowl, and used brass paper fasteners as rivets for the venting ducts. He really got into it, even using battery-operated lights up top in the bowl. But you don't have to have that kind of technical know-how or invest that kind of time to make a cool robot. Get creative with boxes and cardboard to create a great shape. First, spray paint the whole box silver and let dry. Then paint on lights, buttons, and rivets.

RODEO KING

Cut the bull, city-slicker . . . It's time to put your lasso to work. For this costume, you'll need a bandanna, jeans, a cowboy shirt (denim or any other color—anything with pearly snap buttons and/or embroidered pockets), cowboy boots, and, of course, a piece of rope with a loop tied at the end.

SCOTCH AND SODA

Did someone order a **scotch and soda?** Bet they weren't expecting some character in a plaid kilt and bagpipes, with soda cans duct taped to his clothes.

A SHOE STEPPING IN BUBBLEGUM

On more than one occasion, we've had to ask ourselves why some people feel the need to spit their wads of sticky chewing gum right out on the sidewalk. And never is it a more perplexing question than when you yourself have planted your foot directly in the gob, connecting the curb to the left heel of your favorite pair of boots by a stringy, germy strand of chewed-up Bubbalicious. Unfortunately, although this costume does address that mystery of the modern era, it does not answer the decades-old question, "Why not the trash can on the corner?" All you need is lots of pink clothing and a clean sneaker. Cover yourself head to toe in pink, including your face, if you've got some pink face paint handy (pink blush will work in a pinch). Next, tie the laces of your sneaker under your chin, as if the sneaker were an old-fashioned bonnet. Pedestrians unite!

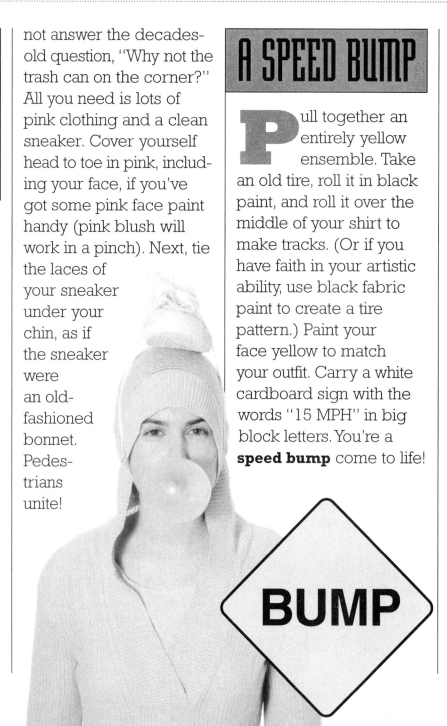

A SPEED BUMP

Pull together an entirely yellow ensemble. Take an old tire, roll it in black paint, and roll it over the middle of your shirt to make tracks. (Or if you have faith in your artistic ability, use black fabric paint to create a tire pattern.) Paint your face yellow to match your outfit. Carry a white cardboard sign with the words "15 MPH" in big block letters. You're a **speed bump** come to life!

BUMP

TELEVISION AND REMOTE CONTROL

You'll need two large boxes for this getup: one taller, one wider. Paint the taller one (the remote control) black, and cut out holes for your arms and head so it can be worn like an awkward jumper. Then glue "buttons" to the front— sponges cut in half and painted black work well. In silver pen, write the name of a television manufacturer, such as Sony or Panasonic, on the upper right-hand corner. The wider box should be painted to resemble a television set with the same company name written in the lower left-hand corner. For your screen image, collage pictures from entertainment mags like *People* or *Entertainment Weekly.*

STATIC CLING

Someone call in the spray guard! Attach stray socks and undies to your outfit by safety-pinning them from the inside (so you don't see most of the pin), bunch your skirt or pants up, and hairspray your hair in a vertical direction.

TORNADO

Some people joke that it's easy to deduce what room Bridie's been in, because it looks like it's been hit by a **tornado** (a mild exaggeration). Hey, when someone gives us criticism, we see costume potential: To go as a natural disaster, wear a torn flannel shirt and torn jeans, and stick miniature cows, houses, and trees to various parts of your outfit. Whip your hair into a windblown beehive. Don't forget to clean up after yourself when you're done getting ready.

TRAFFIC LIGHT

You'll stop traffic in this super-easy getup. All you need is a black turtleneck and black pants. Cut out 6-inch circles from green, yellow, and red construction paper or felt. Stick them to your shirt with washable glue or double-sided tape. If you're feeling really bossy, wear sunglasses, a white glove, and a whistle around your neck, and tell people when they can stop and go.

TUBE O' TOOTHPASTE

What you'll need to become a **tube o' toothpaste:** An extra-long white pillowcase, a small white pleated lampshade, fabric paint or markers, ribbon, a hot glue gun. Slit the seams on the pillowcase just for your head and arms to fit through. Paint the logo of your favorite toothpaste brand on one side of the case. Wear a white turtleneck underneath. Hot glue the ends of the ribbon to two opposing points on the lampshade so you can wear the shade securely as a bonnet.

TWO TREES AND A HAMMOCK

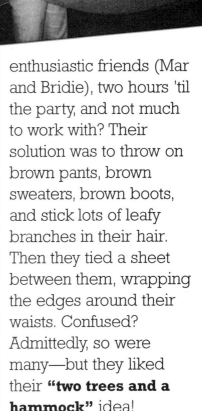

One Halloween, not too long ago, a group of friends—let's call them Bridie's college roommates—agreed to dress up as the Spice Girls. Admittedly, it was not a particularly inspired costume idea, and, in fact, as the 31st drew nigh, it ended up not inspiring three of the five to dress up at all.

So then there were two. And since, at the time, it seemed *wrong* to break up the Spice Girls, a new costume idea had to be hatched, and *tout de suite!* What to do with two enthusiastic friends (Mar and Bridie), two hours 'til the party, and not much to work with? Their solution was to throw on brown pants, brown sweaters, brown boots, and stick lots of leafy branches in their hair. Then they tied a sheet between them, wrapping the edges around their waists. Confused? Admittedly, so were many—but they liked their **"two trees and a hammock"** idea!

ULTRA PREP

You know the type. Chino pants or Nantucket "reds," ribbon belt with whales on it, polo shirt, cable-knit sweater, loafers with no socks. Useful props: a cell phone, tennis racket or polo mallet, a gin and tonic. Girls can don just about the same thing, focusing on pink and green and perhaps substituting a Lilly Pulitzer skirt for the pants.

THE UNWELCOME HOUSEGUEST

To paraphrase Ben Franklin, some guests are like fish: Keep 'em around too long, and they start to stink. Although some guests wear out their welcome in as little as fifteen minutes, many don't seem to take the hint that it's time to leave even after fifteen *days*. Hope you don't have one in your life (they're worse than termites). The first red flag is the unannounced arrival—with enough luggage for a year. It's a hassle, but try to tote around as much baggage as you can. Wrap two pet snakes around your neck. Carry a baby doll, ideally one with a built-in scream capacity, and a stuffed dog or parrot.

UPS WORKER

Dress all in brown, and attach a stuffed dog to your pant leg using a hot glue gun (be prepared to sacrifice both the stuffed animal and the pants). Carry a clipboard and a few packages, and you're a **UPS worker.** Dress in blue to be a **postal worker.**

USED-CAR SALESMAN

Everybody *loves* a **used-car salesman,** right? Maybe not—but even pleasant people can dream of being as unctuous and pushy as possible for one night. Combine your boldest, widest tie with a checked jacket and a striped shirt, or wear a loud pattern without a tie. Brown polyester pants, oily hair, and a huge contract (with X's all over it), and you're ready to make the sale. Dangle car keys in front of friends' faces and reiterate endlessly how much they're going to "love this beauty" you've got picked out for them.

WORLD CHAMPION POKER PLAYER

Go for a royal flush! All it takes is a poker face and, if you're modeling yourself on Dutch Boyd, an upside-down visor, sunglasses, and a flashy button-down, short-sleeved shirt.

AN X-RAY MACHINE

This is an easy one, no bones about it: Buy two large pieces of black posterboard to make a sand-wich board (see page 174). On the front and back, paint the torso, arms, and thighs of a skeleton with white paint (or glue on a picture of a skeleton). Wear all black. You're see-through!

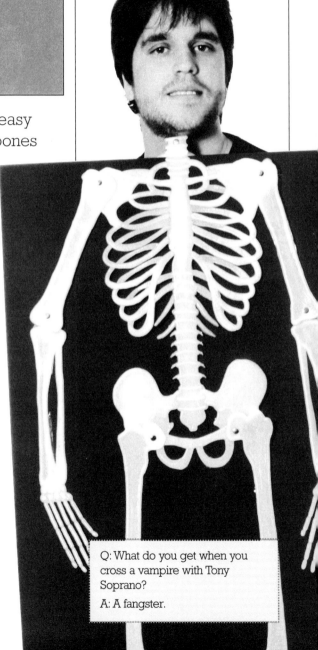

Q: What do you get when you cross a vampire with Tony Soprano?

A: A fangster.

Grosser than Gross

In every crowd, there's at least one person who goes for the "eew" factor (there's usually a whole lot of empty space around him or her). If your goal is to turn your friends green (and *not* with envy), we have a few suggestions for you.

DR. BEN DOVER, SURPRISED PROCTOLOGIST. You'll need some medical scrubs or a white labcoat, a stethoscope, latex gloves, and whatever other medical props you can find. You'll also have to pick up a container or two of chocolate pudding—to smear all over your hands, arms, and the front of your clothing. Instead of making everyone guess what you are —"an MD covered in brown stuff?"—why not let the rest of the party know with a name tag? Just get ready for the gagging when the full mental image comes into focus.

ROADKILL. Throw on your faux fur jacket and cover your head in fake blood so it looks like you've been massively wounded—like, run over. Consider adding some tire tracks to your face.

A ZIT BEING POPPED. Try out John Belushi's *Animal House* antics for yourself this year. First, you'll need to layer up in shades of red, brown, and pink, so pull out anything in that spectrum from your closet. Next, paint your face pink or use pink blush. If you're one of these unlucky souls who gets whiteheads, consider slathering your face with white Desitin. A red or pink cap is the finishing touch. Now head for the kitchen and whip up some mashed potatoes. Cool Whip works, too. Fill a Tupperware container full of the white stuff, tuck it under your arm, and head out into the night. When you arrive at your destination, fill your mouth with mashed potatoes and amble up to your first victim. Tilting his or her head at your multishaded ensemble and chipmunk cheeks, the unsuspecting person will inevitably inquire: "What're *you* supposed to be?" Now's your chance! Squish your cheeks hard enough to force the white stuff out of your mouth. **"A zit being popped!"** you can gleefully exclaim. This is your Clearasil, clear-the-room moment. We can almost guarantee you'll go home alone, but you'll be off the Richter scale of revolting.

The Criminal Element

You can be a law-abiding citizen the other 364 days of the year. On Halloween, it's time to throw the straight and narrow for a little curve.

BURGLAR. Break and enter! We're not suggesting that you *actually* indulge in a life of crime, but dressing the part is totally above-board. All black, with panty hose, a ski mask, or dark makeup and a skullcap. Tiptoe around the party with a bag of loot on your back. Can you carry a television set? If

not, two fistfuls of costume jewelry will suffice. If you don't want to be just any old burglar, put on a little feline makeup (see page 119) and skulk about as a **cat burglar.** Or stuff a few plush toy cats in your sack!

CONVICT. Break free from the chains . . . Take a white sweat suit and use black fabric paint or duct tape to cover it with thick

horizontal stripes. Buy a plastic ball and chain to put around one ankle. Or buy fake hand-cuffs to put around a wrist (for a gruesome effect, pick up a bloody arm from a Halloween shop to dangle from the other cuff). But if you have higher aspirations, add a painter's palette, a French beret, and several large paintbrushes. Now you're using your brain—you're a **con artist.**

GANGSTERS. The off-the-charts success of *The Sopranos* (not to mention the classics, *The Godfather* and *Goodfellas*) should be enough to tell you that **gangsters** are always in. Go old school with a double-breasted pin-striped suit, a black shirt, and a white tie. Don't forget your fedora or the (plastic) machine gun concealed by your side. Is the lady in your life thinking of going as anything other than your **moll?** Tell her to

''fuhgeddaboudit.''
Think Michelle Pfeiffer in *Scarface* or Sharon Stone in *Casino:* slinky black gown, fur, diamonds (or rhinestones).

POLICE OUTLINE.
Return to the scene of the crime with this clever costume. Dress all in black, with a line of white tape outlining the edges of your body. If you have a

significant other, get him or her to dress up as a **convict** (see opposite).

WILD WEST OUTLAW.
Stick 'em up! You'll be the meanest, baddest, fastest gunslinger in town if you wear black jeans, black cowboy boots, a white shirt, and a black vest or jacket. Wear a western-style belt and sling on a holster with two pistols. Don't forget your black cowboy hat and your grimace.

Recycling Effort

Hand-Me-Downs

There are those of us who prefer the familiar and who master—and refuse to deviate from—one costume. Still, there comes a time when J. Lo will *not* do (our friend Zani is about to celebrate her third anniversary as the Latina diva). Sometimes change is good. Here are a few ideas for making your old, has-been costumes into something new and fresh.

Last Year's Costume	This Year's Costume	How to Pull It Off
Clown	Jester	Lose the wig; add a cap and wand
Princess	Fairy	Add a wand and some wings
Blushing Bride	Frankenstein's Bride	Add some ghoulish makeup, blood, knife
Dracula	Zorro	Shorten your cape; add a mask and sword
Ghost	A Greek God	Turn your white sheet into a toga; add a garland
Devil	Lady in Red	Lose the horns; add a rose
Gypsy Girl	Carmen Miranda	Add a basket of fruit to your head

TINKERBELL
page 250

DALMATION
page 253

CLOWN
page 243

CHAPTER FOURTEEN

Nursery Rhymes, Fairy Tales, and Costumes for the Young at Heart

Celebrate your inner child with these timeless costumes, or dress your little ones as characters from their favorite stories.

PRINCESS
page 245

ALADDIN

Aladdin needs billowy pants and (optional) shirt, and a colorful, open vest. Add a bright satin sash tied around the waist and some inconspicuous moccasins, and it's a look that'll open doors. Tote along a "magic lamp"— any small brass teapot will do.

BERT'S RUBBER DUCKIE

This is Bridie's younger brother, Dan, in his third-grade school play. He played **Bert's Rubber Duckie** from Sesame Street. Mom, who designed the costume, saw nothing wrong with her son looking like this in front of the entire school. What you need: orange or yellow tights. A yellow leotard (Capezio sells most of the colors in the rainbow. If you can't find one, substitute a yellow sweat suit). Cover your yellow base with yellow feathers (check with your local sewing goods retailer). Cover your sneakers with orange socks, rolled down. You should also have a pair of yellow rubber gloves and a yellow shower cap. Carry a bathtub back scrubber. Lastly, let's face it: it was the indigo-blue eye shadow smeared over each eye that really made Dan's costume memorable for Bridie, and for most of their school. Apply liberally.

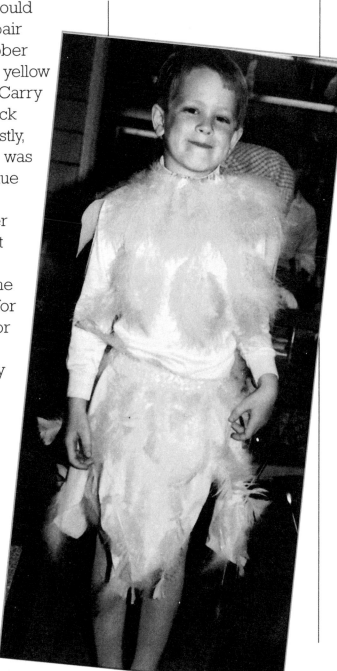

CINDERELLA (BEFORE AND AFTER)

Talk about a fairy-tale makeover. One friend dresses as **Cinderella-in-rags** (the "before" shot): tattered and torn clothing, black ballet slippers, a mop, a pail, big patches over a plain skirt . . . in short, the trod-upon look. Wear a faded rag or bandanna around your hair. The other friend dresses as **Cinderella-at-the-ball:** ball gown, hair in an elegant updo, a choker, and, of course, those famous glass slippers (clear plastic or silver works just fine).

Keep checking your watch—you have a strict midnight curfew.

CLOWN

Everyone loves 'em! And there are so many different ways to make a great **clown** costume. One suggestion: Wear parachute pants and a colorful top, as mis-matched as possible, and add bright suspenders. Think about buying big floppy plastic shoes, a red rubber nose, and the requisite fluorescent orange wig. If you have a rubber chicken, a whoopee cushion, a horn, a small tricycle, and/or a flower that squirts water, bring them along.

If you want to go all the way, paint your face white, give yourself a red, oversized "smile" that circles outside your lips by about half an inch. Paint your cheeks with a shape (rainbows, hearts, stars, etc.). With purple or blue face paint, add a long triangle above and below each eye.

DENNIS THE MENACE

Poor, long-suffering Mr. Wilson. He seemed to get some rest and respite from his irksome young neighbor after the eponymous 1960s sitcom went off the air—only to have his trials and tribulations revived in the 1990s movie remake. Have a little blond whippersnapper of your own? Set Junior loose as **Dennis** this Halloween: All he needs is a pair of overalls, a striped shirt, Converse sneakers, a slingshot in the front pocket, and, of course, a few freckles and the huge cowlick on the back of his head.

GOLDILOCKS

Hair is essential to the costume, of course. You'll need blond ringlets, tied up with blue bows. Wear a blue-and-white-checked dress with an apron, plus standard-issue little-girl footwear: white knee socks and black Mary Janes. You'll remember that little **Goldilocks** was guilty of breaking and entering the home of the innocent Bear family. But her crime spree didn't end there. After scarfing down most of their delicious porridge and breaking their furniture, she was finally exhausted by her own naughtiness and crawled into each and every bed in the house before nodding off in Baby Bear's. Capture these elements by toting an empty cereal bowl, a baby blanket, and a stuffed teddy bear.

THREE BLIND MICE

For an inseparable trio. The rodent uniform: gray sweatpants and hooded sweatshirts with gray felt ears attached, mouse noses (store-bought, or draw black tips and whiskers), and long pink tails. Sunglasses and canes complete the look.

PETER PAN

A perfect costume for a boy who won't grow up: Dress all in green—tights, a long T-shirt, and shorts. Cut your shirt-sleeves and hem in a jagged, zigzag pattern. Drape yourself in a vine for a leafy effect. Wear a feather in a green cap. Carry a toy knife and pixie dust. Jump off a few chairs and encourage others to "think happy thoughts."

PRINCESS

What little girl doesn't dream of being royalty? Standard **princess** garb: a long, flowing gown (perhaps her nightgown will do?) and either a tiara or a pointy, pastel-colored hat (poster board fashioned into a cone and stapled shut, decorated with shiny stickers and glitter), with a billowing chiffon scarf or ribbons attached to the tip.

Princess Variations

Princesses are lovely, but they're a dime a dozen. Go to the old fairy tales to customize your royal look.

FROG PRINCESS. Haven't found the right man yet? Go out and about as the **Frog Princess**—carry around a golden ball and a stuffed frog. Kiss the frog repeatedly throughout the night, and maybe he'll turn into your Prince Charming.

THE PRINCESS AND THE PEA. Have trouble sleeping? Then you're ready to step out as the princess from the **Princess and the Pea.** Wear a sleeping mask pushed up on your forehead, dark circles drawn under your eyes. Every once in a while, complain that it feels like you've been sleeping on a bed of rocks.

RAPUNZEL. If you have long, long, *long* blond hair, you're a natural for **Rapunzel.** (Otherwise, buy a wig.) Create a window frame out of a large cardboard box and paint the box to resemble stones. Pose inside the frame, and don't be afraid to let your hair down.

RUMPELSTILTSKIN. Keep your hands busy as the princess who gets more than a little help from the odd **Rumpelstiltskin.** The handful of straw in one of your pockets is a testament to the impossible task ahead of you. The spool of gold thread in the other, however, proves how much you've accomplished.

SLEEPING BEAUTY. Do your friends complain that you sleep your life away? Well, **Sleeping Beauty,** it's time to prove them right. Show up with a pillow in one hand and a sleeping mask pushed up onto your forehead à la the Princess and the Pea costume (no dark circles for you, though—you haven't had any trouble sleeping). If you're overcome with the need to nap, find a couch or a comfy chair.

SNOW WHITE. All you need is raven-colored hair, blood-red lips, and skin as white as snow. Carry a shiny, polished apple.

JACK FROST

Brrr . . . Do you feel a draft? Your **Jack Frost** costume personifies the winter chill with icy blue skin, blue lips, icicle hair (silver spray, draped and braided with tinsel), blue clothing with tinsel draped over every possible inch. Bring your snowman friend for added authenticity.

JACK AND JILL

Jack and *Jill* went *up the hill, to fetch a pail of water.* A cute idea for two kids: Jill wears a dress, perhaps with an apron, and carries an empty bucket. Jack wears a little dented, broken crown (take a strip of cardboard and cover with tin foil, with a spiked top).

JACK JUMPS OVER THE CANDLESTICK

Simple as a children's limerick: Wear a name tag saying "My name is Jack," and carry a candlestick. When people ask what you are, place the candlestick on the ground and jump over it. Wear something typically youthful, like a pair of overalls.

LITTLE BO PEEP

This is an idea we over-"herd." Wear a big skirt with petticoats, a frilly apron, a bonnet, and curls —and a tall, candy cane—shaped crook for rounding up those non-existent sheep. Carry a poster around with a cartoon drawing of a sheep, and the words "Have you seen . . ." underneath.

LITTLE BOY BLUE

LITTLE RED RIDING HOOD

Super easy. Dress all in blue and carry a horn.

This is an easy, fun costume for a big or little girl: Dress all in red, including a red cape or hooded sweatshirt (for a modern adaptation). Carry a picnic basket. A parent can dress up as the **Wolf** in all black and brown—a fur or faux fur coat works especially well— plus ears and fangs. Or wear a gray wig, a nightgown, and glasses, and you're the wolf posing as the **grandmother.**

MISS MARY MACK

She's all dressed in black (we suggest a dress or T-shirt and skirt combo), with silver buttons sewn down the back. Make oversized buttons out of cardboard covered with aluminum foil. Stick them to your back with double-sided tape or loosely sew them onto your shirt.

When people find out who you are, they'll want to recite the whole rhyme from memory. In case they fail, you should be prepared to finish it. Here's a refresher.

Miss Mary Mack, Mack, Mack,
All dressed in black, black, black,
With silver buttons, buttons,

buttons,
Sewn down her back, back, back.
She asked her mother, mother, mother
For 50 cents, cents, cents,
To see the elephants, elephants, elephants
Jump over the fence, fence, fence.
They jumped so high, high, high,
They reached the sky, sky, sky,
And they didn't come back, back, back
'Til the fourth of July, ly, ly.

TINKERBELL

Who can resist everyone's favorite fairy? Wear a little green dress (preferably with jagged edges at the hem and sleeves). Affix gossamer wings to your back (see page 5) and wear green slippers with lighter green pom-poms on them (or your best approximation). If you like, pile your hair on top of your head. Wave your sparkly wand and sprinkle fairy dust wherever you go.

Party Games for the Wee Ones

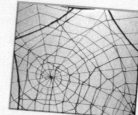

Hosting the little ones this year? Here are a few fun activities that'll keep the crew temporarily distracted from their candy.

Where's My Mummy?

Divide kids into teams of three (one mummy, one wrapper, one unwrapper). Hand each team one roll of toilet paper. When you say "Go," the wrapper on each team wraps up the designated mummy with the entire roll, careful not to let it rip. (Any team that rips the paper must start over with a new roll—but only one do-over per team allowed!) Once that's done, the unwrapper immediately steps up to the plate and begins carefully unwrapping the mummy—again without ripping the paper. The team that finishes first is the winner.

Oh, the Tangled Webs We Weave

All you need for this game are a few small balls of yarn, about 30 to 40 feet each, preferably in Halloween colors. Pair the kids off and stand them in two lines about 5 feet apart, with teammates facing each other. At your signal to go, teammates begin tossing the ball of yarn to each other, wrapping once around themselves, and tossing back. The first team to finish their yarn wins.

Monster Anatomy 101

Here's a treat, or a trick rather, for the kids. Devote a corner of a room or a whole room of the house to a concentration of booby-trapped, ghost-infested horror. (Okay, so adults will probably enjoy this, too.) Hang extra ghosts and tons of crepe paper streamers from the ceiling to give this area a claustrophobic feeling. Keep the eerie music playing, cut the lights almost entirely, and place some extra dry ice around to keep things foggy and mysterious.

Assemble four boxes with lids, deep enough to fit a bowl inside. Then cut a hole in each lid, so a hand can fit inside. Next, fill four bowls with "monster parts." We recommend the following: Usher your guest, whatever their age may be, over to the **"operating table."** Ask them to close their eyes, then slowly place their hands into different bowls, telling them they're touching the following contents:

- **"Eyeballs"—peeled grapes, or a less time-consuming alternative, canned lychee fruit**
- **"Human ribs"—barbecue ribs**
- **"Toe jam"—peanut butter, cottage cheese, and applesauce**
- **"A human heart"—warm pudding tied in a plastic bag**
- **"A human brain"—a whole head of cauliflower rubbed with vegetable oil (a less messy alternative is a "preserved brain" stored in water)**
- **"Unraveled intestines"— cooked black linguine**
- **"Preserved ears"—dried apricots**

Have the kids guess what they're touching . . . once they're done squealing. Remember to keep damp paper towels or wet wipes at the end of your assembly line. Be sure not to miss one kid, or you'll find sticky fingerprints all over the house.

BABY, IT'S YOU

You don't have to be walking to enjoy Halloween. Here are some costume ideas for the Under-one set that are guaranteed to make passersby say, "*Soooooo* cute!"

An Acorn and Tree.

Dress baby all in brown and wrap her in a brown blanket. On her head, a little brown cap with a "stem" sewn on (brown felt or pipe cleaner). For Mom or Dad's part, dress in brown and pin green felt leaves (preferably in the shape of an oak leaf) to your arms and shoulders. Pin more leaves to a brown cap or wrap a leafy artificial vine (available at craft shops) around your hair. When it comes to Halloween spirit, the **acorn** doesn't fall far from the **tree.**

Button.

Think that little one of yours is as cute as a **button?** He'll look even cuter dressed as one this Halloween. It's a cinch to make: Cut two big circles (big enough to fit baby inside, like a mini sleeping bag) out of brightly colored felt. Sew up the sides, leaving ample room for a head opening. In the middle of the circles, draw or paste on four smaller black circles (to look like the face of a button).

Candy Corn.

If your baby's pretty sweet, a **candy corn** makes for a toothsome costume. First, you're going to create the orange and yellow base. You'll need about two yards of orange felt and a yard of yellow felt. Lay the baby on the orange felt with her head sticking above the top. Then, leaving a generous amount of kicking room, fold the felt up to double it. Remove baby from the felt and trim off any excess from the top. Cut the doubled-over felt into a generous trapezoid (the triangle of a candy corn, minus the white top). Then cut a wide strip of yellow felt and use craft glue or a hot glue gun to attach it to the bottom of the costume. Turn the costume inside out, and sew (or staple) each side together three-quarters of the way up. (If stapling, fold duct tape over the stapled seams to keep them from poking or chafing the little wearer.) Put baby in and use diaper pins to close. (If you're feeling crafty, sew a button on each side of the front and cut buttonholes on the back). Ideally, baby is wearing an orange or yellow shirt. Last step: Add a little white knit hat. The cutest candy corn you ever saw. For an easier variation of this costume, simply dress your little one in yellow pants, an orange shirt, and a white hat.

Dalmatian. There are 101 reasons to dress your little darling as a spotty **dalmatian** this year. Get a pair of white pants and a white

hooded sweatshirt. Either glue on black felt dots or use a fabric marker to draw them on. Sew two white ears— spotted, naturally— onto the top of her hood. On her face, draw some whiskers, a pink nose, and more black dots—and she'll be the pick of the litter.

Dinosaur. Another favorite: Buy a green sweatsuit or get your hands on any green shirt and pants combination (if you don't find a hooded sweatshirt, pick up a green cap of some sort). Then cut yellow and green sponges on the

diagonal and pin them all the way down her back, starting at her head. For full effect, add a light layer of green face paint.

Mini-Me. Perfect for a dad and his little bald baby. Dress up in matching outfits, preferably all white or all gray. Dad puts on a bald cap (see page 75) and carries Junior around in a sling carrier: Dr. Evil and Mini-Me from the *Austin Powers* movies.

Pea in a Pod. Dress your little one up in all green (green hood, green pajamas) and wrap him or her in a green blanket. A precious **Pea in a Pod.**

Snug as a Bug in a Rug. Dress Junior up as a little insect: green pj's, a headband with antennae. Then wrap him in a very soft, very clean, furry bath mat (ideally not the kind with rubber on one side).

Stocking Stuffer. For baby's first Halloween, comfort and warmth are key. She or he will have plenty of time for gossamer fairy costumes and spider-man suits down the line. Measure baby from collarbone to toes and double the number. Buy enough of the softest red faux fur you can find at your local fabric store to make a roomy stocking. If it has white faux fur, buy enough of that to trim one top of the stocking. At home, on the scratch side of the red fabric, trace a stocking with chalk, giving Junior plenty of room for leg movement. Then cut along the lines, and use that cutout to make a duplicate. Sew the two sides together, faux fur facing out. Glue the white trim along the top of your custom-made stocking. (If you don't have white fur a swatch of cotton from a roll will do fine.) Put a green bow on your little one's head, and you and your most adorable **stocking stuffer** are ready to celebrate Halloween for the first time.

Train Conductor. Repeat after us . . . ''I think I can come up with a fun Halloween costume for Junior . . . I think I can . . . I think I can . . . '' Here's the perfect one for a kid who loves *The Little Engine that Could.* You're on the right track with overalls, a white turtleneck, and a conductor's hat (in a pinch, a blue-and-white striped cap works fine), a train whistle, and a miniature train to tote around.

Q: Why did the skeleton go to the party alone?
A: He had no body to go with.

What To Wear When You're Expecting

Expecting a little critter? Don't stay at home on Halloween! Wear one of these costume ideas and flaunt your new "accessory"—your beautiful maternal belly!

■ **Bun in the Oven.** If you have the time and you're feeling creative, draw or paint an oven on a white T-shirt. Draw a loaf of bread baking inside the oven (seen through the window on the door). Let people know you've got something baking: "It's almost ready!"

■ **Mama Kangaroo.** Wear all brown from head to toe, and add brown mini-bunny ears (two pieces of tear-shaped brown felt, with smaller pink cut-outs glued inside, attached to a headband) and a long brown tail. Sew a pocket of brown material onto your belly and make baby kangaroo ears out of felt so they peep out, hinting at the cutie-pie within.

■ **Miraculous Materni-T.** Transform a long white maternal T-shirt into a great costume by using fabric markers or paint to draw a pumpkin, basketball, beach ball, or any other round object that comes to mind, over your belly. Hold your belly so that it looks like you're carrying the object. (Tell your hostess you have been carrying this pumpkin around for six and a half months, just so you could bring it to her Halloween party!)

■ **A Mummy.** Start by dressing all in black. Partially wrap yourself in mummy gear (see page 15), but don't cover yourself completely. (And don't wrap too tightly!) Leave some black clothing showing, and pin the wrap so some of the ends dangle. When you talk to anyone, rub your belly and tell them you're "going to be a mummy."

Top 10 Family-Friendly Flicks

The old struggle at Blockbuster . . . Your little ones want to rent the gruesome *Nightmare on Elm Street,* but you know they'll be scared out of their wits. The compromise? Check out any of the following movies. Your kids will be entertained in the Halloween spirit, and they'll be able to sleep at night.

Hocus Pocus. Bette Midler, Kathy Najimy, and Sarah Jessica Parker play three feisty, witchy sisters back to seek revenge on the current-day inhabitants of Salem, Massachusetts, the town that sent them to the gallows three centuries earlier. Funny and fast moving.

The Addams Family. Inspired by the small-screen sitcom, this PG-13 flick will get the whole family into a creepy Halloween spirit. Anjelica Huston is *goth*-gorgeous as Morticia, and Christina Ricci is a perfect misfit as Wednesday.

It's the Great Pumpkin, Charlie Brown! A perennial childhood classic—Halloween doesn't feel like Halloween until you've caught a viewing. Linus waits loyally for the arrival of the Great Pumpkin while his Peanuts pals trick-or-treat . . . Will his faith be rewarded?

The Nightmare Before Christmas. Tim Burton's inventive stop-motion, animated film tells the tale of Jack Skellington, the mayor of Halloweentown, who has become enchanted by Christmas. Great tunes.

Beetlejuice. Michael Keaton stars as the loudmouthed Beetlejuice in this zany, high-spirited comedy about a ghost couple trying to scare off the new owners of their home. Winona Ryder and Alec Baldwin also shine.

Casper. A widower (Bill Pullman) and his daughter (Christina Ricci) move into a house already inhabited by Casper the Friendly Ghost. The interaction between the live actors and the computer-generated Casper can be awkward, but it's still a kid favorite.

High Spirits. Peter O'Toole tries to salvage his finances by passing off his heavily mortgaged castle in Ireland as a "haunted" tourist attraction. But when he makes a show of his made-up ghosts for his American guests (played by Steve Guttenberg and Beverly D'Angelo), a couple whose marriage is on the fritz, he ends up stirring up the castle's *real* ghosts, including one played by Darryl Hannah.

The Witches. This adaptation of the Roald Dahl classic is a must-see. Anjelica Huston stars as The Grand High Witch. Creatively done, but scary at moments.

Labyrinth. Sarah (Jennifer Connelly) wishes that goblins would take her baby brother away. They do, and Sarah sets out to rescue him from the Goblin King (David Bowie). With the exception of Bowie, the goblins and the myriad characters are all puppets designed by Jim Henson and his team.

The Halloween Tree. This animated favorite, based on a story by Ray Bradbury, explores the magic of Halloween throughout the ages.

Index

Acknowledgments

We'd like to thank our agent, Daniel Greenberg, and our editor, Jennifer Griffin, for seeing our potential and taking a chance on first-time authors. We'd especially like to thank Cindy Schoen, Margot Herrera, Micah Hales, Aaron Clendening, Grace Turato, Leora Kahn, and David Miller, who improved this book immeasurably through their close reading, thoughtful responses, and tireless work.

We'd like to extend our gratitude to the following people for their invaluable contributions:
Jonathan Aghravi, Stacey Alper, Barbaralynn Altdorfer, Ralph A. Attanasia, James Bessoir, Robert Bessoir, Patrick Borelli, Ridgely Brode, Emily Brodsky, Eric Brown, Ford Brown, Marisa Noel Brown, Hampton Carney, Nicholas Caruso, Dorothy Cavanagh, Mariah Chase, Melanie Charlton, Dan Clark, Grace Clark, Tom Clark, Kevin Davidson, Lauren Davis, Shannon Delage, Cecilia De Sola, Carolina Dorson, Elizabeth Doty, Billy Duffey, Maureen Duffey, Rudy Duran, Stephanie Ercklentz, Julie Feldman, Christopher Fisher, Elizabeth Gaynor, Vivian Ghazarian, Joy Gotthardt, Zani Gugelmann, Stephanie Harris, Emilia Hernandez, Carmen Herrera, Luke Janka, Marta Jaremko, Fatimah Khan, Samantha Kain, Maggie Katz, Erin Leopold, Katie Lewis, Amy Lipman, Molly Macdonald, Melanie Macleod, Susan Macleod, Samuel Madden, Fitz Maloney, Katie Maloney, Matt Maloney, Elizabeth Meigher, David Miller, Vivian Mora, Daria Natan, Franz Nicolay, Megan Nicolay, Andra Olenik, Dove Pedlosky, Ogden Phipps, Alexander Powers, Eileen Pybus, Rebecca Schiff, Robyn Schwartz, Tod Seelie, Kirsten Steglich, Stormy Stokes, Lindley Tilghman, Elaine Tom, Lucy Toole, Robert Vargas, Alexandra Wilkis, Paul Wilmot, Andra Winokur, Rick Wolff, and Laura Zukerman.

We would like to thank the following for additional photographic contributions:
AP/Wide World Photos: page 78 (left); **Culver Pictures, Inc.:** page 60 (left), page 76, page 105 (left), page 119 (all 6 on right), page 142 (left), page 172 (right), page 201 (bottom right); **Dietrich Gehring:** page 139 (middle left and top right), page 197, page 203 (middle), page 208 (right), page 210, page 211 (middle), page 215 (all); **Getty Images:** page 86, page 75 (middle), page 196 (bottom), page 215, page 231; **Globe Photos:** Color insert page 5 (middle), page 61, page 133 (right), page 136 (left), page 137 (bottom), page 138 (left), page 143 (right), page 160 (left), page 167 (left); **Hulton Archive/Getty Images:** page 85, both; **J. Murphy/Globe Photos:** page 127 (top right), page 135 (left); **Library of Congress:** page 82 (right); **Mary Evans Picture Library:** page 18; **Photofest:** Color insert page 4 (second from left), page 1 (bottom left), page 19, page 54 (right), page 87 (bottom left), page 88 (top), page 100 (left), page 101 (both), page 103, page 105 (right), page 106 (left), page 110 (right), page 127 (right), page 132 (right), page 144 (right), page 148 (left), page 149 (left), page 151 (right), page 177 (top left), page 181 (bottom), page 194, page 256 (bottom right); **Vario Press/Imapress/Globe Photos:** page 129 (bottom); **Wonderfile:** page 83, page 161 (right).